## Praise for We Are Their Voices

"*We Are Their Voices* focuses the reader's attention where it should be—on the life of each victim, rather than on the perpetrator—and on the devastating loss and unique grief of each survivor who loved them."

—Kathleen Garcia
Former Chairwoman of NJ Coalition
for Homicide Survivors;
Founder of South Jersey Survivors
of Violent Crime (SJSVC)

"*We Are Their Voices* gives us an opportunity to express our experiences and emotions after the traumatic loss of our loved ones. I will always celebrate my daughter's life, and this book will certainly help keep her memory alive."

—Lynn McMahon
Mother of Kristen Laurite

"Although the homicide victim's voice is stilled, the voices of those left behind are not. They may question their faith, seek answers about the circumstances of the crime and details about the perpetrator, rail against the limitations of the criminal justice system and above all, cry out for justice for their loved one.

Patricia Goebel and those whose stories are told within *We Are Their Voices, Remembering Our Murdered Loved Ones* share with us the almost unbearable depths of pain, anguish, anger and grief experienced when a loved one has been murdered. Complicated by the involvement of the criminal justice system if a perpetrator has been identified, apprehended, and prosecuted, the victim/survivors' ability to deal with these emotions is challenged on a daily basis. When a homicide goes unsolved, the frustration and torment suffered by the victim's loved ones are unimaginable.

Those who read this book will hear the voices of the victims through those left behind to carry on. You will be inspired by the courage of survivors who attend every court appearance representing their loved one; the persistence of those parents who keep their children's stories in the media, hoping for a break in their case. You will be humbled by their strength, their resilience and their desire to help others who may be walking a similar path.

Those of us in the Criminal Justice System or other helping professions will never know what these survivors are feeling or going through. It behooves us to ask and to be willing to listen to their stories, as they speak not only for their loved ones but also for themselves, teaching us how best to help them. We owe it to them to ensure that their voices are heard."

—Linda Burkett, M.S.
Victim Witness Coordinator
Camden County Prosecutor's Office

# WE ARE THEIR
# VOICES

# WE ARE THEIR VOICES

## REMEMBERING OUR MURDERED LOVED ONES

# PATRICIA GOEBEL

TATE PUBLISHING
AND ENTERPRISES, LLC

Scripture quotations marked "NIV" are taken from the *Holy Bible, New International Version* ®, Copyright © 1973, 1978, 1984 by International Bible Society. Used by permission of Zondervan Publishing House. All rights reserved.

Scripture quotations marked "Msg" are taken from *The Message*, Copyright © 1993, 1994, 1995, 1996, 2000, 2001, 2002. Used by permission of NavPress Publishing Group. All rights reserved.

Scripture quotations marked "CEV" are from the *Holy Bible; Contemporary English Version,* Copyright © 1995, Barclay M. Newman, ed., American Bible Society. Used by permission. All rights reserved.

The opinions expressed by the author are not necessarily those of Tate Publishing, LLC.

Published by Tate Publishing & Enterprises, LLC

127 E. Trade Center Terrace | Mustang, Oklahoma 73064 USA
1.888.361.9473 | www.tatepublishing.com

Tate Publishing is committed to excellence in the publishing industry. The company reflects the philosophy established by the founders, based on Psalm 68:11,

*"The Lord gave the word and great was the company of those who published it."*

Book design copyright © 2012 by Tate Publishing, LLC. All rights reserved.
*Cover design by Matias Alasagas*
*Interior design by Jomar Ouano*

Published in the United States of America

ISBN: 978-1-62024-732-7
Law / Criminal Law / General
12.12.12

# DEDICATION

For Stephen R. Goebel: When you were born, I told you I would never let any harm come to you.

# ACKNOWLEDGMENTS

As I navigated the criminal justice process following Steve's murder, I knew my grief must have an outlet. If I felt this way, surely other survivors of murder victims out there felt the same, since we all experience despair and frustration, either in the courtroom or in trying to understand why our loved one's murder has become a cold case. This book was created to give a voice to our murdered loved ones. Its message also extends to the criminal justice system.

From the inception of *We Are Their Voices*, I have had invaluable assistance. In my personal experience with grief, shortly after Stephen's murder, Kathy Garcia—founder of the Center for Traumatic Grief (CTG) and aunt of a murder victim—came into my life. Kathy has been a tireless champion of victim's rights. In fact, she had a major impact in seeing the passage of the Crime Victims Rights Amendment to the New Jersey State Constitution.

Joe Gorman, LCSW and certified grief counselor for CTG, helped the sun shine again for me. Without Joe's guidance, patience, and authentic Irish brand of humor, I would still be muddling through each day trying to overcome Post Traumatic Stress Disorder

(PTSD). Joe's sessions, both individual and group at CTG, provided the foundation for recovery for many of us who had been thrown into a situation we would never wish on anyone. Rich Pompelio—former chief of the Victims of Crime Compensation Board (VCCB), as well as current director of the New Jersey Crime Victims Law Center, father of a murder victim, and an outstanding activist for victim's rights—has been a valued advisor throughout the creation of *We Are Their Voices*. Keeping in mind the legal considerations of writing such a book, the competent advice of Moorestown Attorney Swati Kothari played a crucial role in the creation of *We Are Their Voices*. I also thank my teaching colleagues for continuing to ask me about *my book*. Your compassion and encouragement helped move it from planning to reality.

From the moment I realized my son was dead, I understood on some semiconscious level that many different people and entities would become part of my *new normal*. The justice community—prosecutors, detectives, and investigators—have all become second nature in my daily thoughts. As the days, weeks, and months wore on, I hung onto their every contact, relying on them to keep me informed of any new developments. To this end, the Victim-Witness Advocacy unit of the prosecutor's office, headed by Linda Burkett, is charged with being a liaison to co-victims. Linda's compassion and care—calling, sitting in court each time with us, getting answers to difficult questions, and finally, devoting several hours while I painstakingly pored over

Stephen's entire file—gave me a competent friend/protector to lean on when the sun refused to shine. As each court proceeding took place, Linda settled the dark clouds in their place and helped us to stay sane.

*We Are Their Voices* would not have been written without its contributors—the loved ones of murder victims. This book was eight years in consideration and two years in the actual writing. Every moment of it has been a combination of the toughest, most emotional, most love-filled project I could ever have imagined. To ask survivors of murder victims to open their loved ones to public scrutiny in order to relive the most traumatic event of their lives is not easy. To actually do the reliving and produce a heartfelt submission, painstakingly developed from one's personal anguish, is a true measure of the love and commitment each contributor has for the murdered loved one who can no longer speak for him or her self. With admiration and profound respect for their courage, I acknowledge each of the *We Are Their Voices* contributors, whom you will meet as he or she tells the story of a loved one on the pages of this book.

I also say "thank you" to my family. We have suffered together over the years since Stephen's murder, trying to make sense of something that defies understanding. It has taken its toll on all of us, but we are still here, unwilling to give the murderer one more shred of our lives or sanity. Most important, thank You, God. You hold me up and continue to walk along this road with me each day.

# TABLE OF CONTENTS

*"Don't worry, Mom."*
*"…A good, honest, clean-cut young man"*
*"He taught me so much about life."*
*"Good night baby cakes, love ya."*
*"We pray for peace and justice for Bobby."*
*"She has given me the strength to go back to school…"*
*"He was sent to earth to save his sister…*
*"Brian's Tree represents the circle of life."*

# FOREWORD

## By Rich Pompelio, Esq.—Executive Director, New Jersey Crime Victims Law Center

For over two centuries the criminal justice system in the United States focused solely on the rights of the accused. Victims were not considered to be a part of the justice equation. Their role as witnesses defined their relative importance in the criminal justice process. This one-dimensional application of justice changed dramatically in 1980 when Ronald Reagan became president. President Reagan commissioned a national task force to study the effects of crime on its victims. The findings of the 1982 President's Task Force on Victims of Crime became the spark that ignited the victims' rights revolution that for over three decades has changed the way that we view the criminal justice system.

The chair of the Task Force, Lois Harrington, wrote the following:

> Something has happened in America: Crime has made victims of us all. Awareness of its danger affects the way we think, where we

live, where we go, what we buy, how we raise our children, and the quality of our lives as we age…Somewhere along the way, the system simply treated crime victims with institutional disinterest… The neglect of crime victims is a national disgrace.

The national statistics tell us that someone is murdered every twenty-three minutes. But as we know, one crime or criminal does not produce just one victim. Former Supreme Court Justice David Souter opined in 1991 in the case of *Payne v. Tennessee:*

> Every defendant knows, if endowed with the mental competence for criminal responsibility, that the life he will take by his homicidal behavior is that of a unique person, like himself, and that the person to be killed probably has close associates, *survivors*, who will suffer harms and deprivations from the victim's death. Just as defendants know that they are not faceless human ciphers, they know that their victims are not valueless fungibles; and just as defendants appreciate the web of relationships and dependencies in which they live, they know that their victims are not human islands, but individuals with parents or children, spouses or friends or dependents. Thus, when a defendant chooses to kill or to raise the risk of a victim's death, this choice necessarily relates to a whole human being and threatens an association of others, who may be distinctly hurt.

I have been a crime victim attorney and activist for over two decades. Prior to the 1989 murder of my son, I believed that I knew quite a bit about the criminal justice system. I was wrong; I only knew what I had been taught. One cannot understand the criminal justice process unless he has experienced the frightening predicament of being at its mercy. Victims are thrust into a criminal justice process in which they have few rights, compared to the defendant and where they are oftentimes overwhelmed by fear and loneliness.

The single most frequent question I ask myself before I am about to begin a lecture or training to judges, prosecutors, lawyers, students, and anyone else who will listen to pleas for equal justice for victims is, "How can I make them understand the never-ending struggle that a survivor of homicide endures?" *We Are Their Voices* is so powerful because it is so real. It reminds us that the joy of love and the pain of loss are in direct proportion to each other.

For those who work in the criminal justice system, the cases come and go. But for the victim there is only one case, and it never ends. When someone is killed because of the criminal act of another, there is created a river of grief that will continue to flow until everyone who ever knew the victim is no longer alive. There is no closure, and there can be no true justice for victims. *We Are Their Voices* should be mandatory reading for every law student, prosecutor, and judge. It reminds us that life is ever so fragile and that we cannot take for granted one moment of joy and happiness with our loved ones. Our loved ones never die. While we can no longer physically hold them in our arms; nevertheless, we continue to hold them in our hearts. And through us, their voices will always be heard.

# AUTHOR'S NOTE

"When you are so sorrowful, look into your heart and you shall see that you are weeping for that which has been your delight."

Kahlil Gibran

The following is a collection of the emotions of grief that dominate each survivor's life as the horror of a loved one's murder is relived. There are basic necessities that help co-victims of homicide come to terms with the reality of murder and move from shock through the grieving process. Among these is making sure your loved one is remembered and doing everything in your power to insure that justice is realized for the victim. This book gives a face and voice to each victim and the life each was denied.

How does a survivor go on after a loved one is murdered? How does he or she view the world in the aftermath? This book begins with my son's story. I have asked other co-victims of murder to contribute their loved ones' stories to *We Are Their Voices* as well. We must be their voices: contacting the prosecutor's office for any news, offering rewards, displaying posters, buying space on billboards, being present for court proceedings, making sure that the judge knows we are there, holding candlelight vigils, attending grief counseling sessions, and publishing memorials. We contribute to causes in honor of our loved one's memory; we create scholarships and foundations. And we are telling our loved ones' stories here. Who else can do this? There is no one else to be the victim's voice.

It's very hard to sit in a courtroom during proceedings where the murderer has the right to speak, but as the voice of the victim, we do not. It's tormenting to sit in the courtroom with the murderer's family and witness his father thrusting his fist forward in a show of "stay strong" to his son while my son's body lies in its grave. Each of us has a tale to tell of our loved one. We want you to hear their voices; they want you to hear their voices. We hope this will help you to understand how it is to live this nightmare and still come out sane on the other side of the worst experience of our lives.

If you are reading this as the family member of a murder victim, whether you are a spouse, parent, child or other family member, please know I am truly saddened that your loved one has been taken from you. I pray you will feel love and support around you and that you will experience God's grace as you walk this hardest of journeys. You will sometimes think that grief will consume you; at times, you may feel that you can't go on another moment. It may be helpful at these times to cry, scream, pray, to reflect on pleasant memories and even read the entries in honor of the loved ones included in this book. No one can tell you how long you will grieve, or how to grieve. It is hard work, and does not follow any schedule. There will be times when you may hear a certain song, or see a movie, read a scripture, witness the first butterfly of spring…there are so many grief triggers, and you may fall apart. It's ok to feel this way. No apologies are necessary. If you feel you can't talk to friends or other family about your grief because it makes them feel uncomfortable, well, you are not alone. I've often felt that way. Then, too, some well-meaning people will stop mentioning your loved one for fear that being reminded will hurt you. The truth is that you never "forget" your loved one. And more to the point, keeping his or her memory alive is much more important to you than trying to forget. My hope is that you will realize though we may not have ever met, we know one another's heart and the pain we share is real. I also pray for justice for your loved one, and that our court system will endeavor to understand and respect your need to be your loved one's voice.

Join us as we introduce you to our loved ones—victims of murder. Each life has been cut short. They have been denied life goals: marriage, children, travel, that dream house or special car. They will never work toward a career or do something wonderful for the world. Please hear their voices and remember them… and tell the criminal justice system to do the same.

Stephen Goebel, Christopher Acosta, Shane Hebert, Timothy Clark, Robert Ucciferri, Rachel Dennis, Jarred Neal, Brian Ray Miller, Ronald Allen Fraga, Kristen Laurite, Ruth Angel Hayes, and thousands more... We are their voices.

# INTRODUCTION

Seventy-six stab wounds...every vital organ pierced, lacerated...throat slashed...nearly decapitated.

Our criminal justice system must evolve to allow survivors to speak for those whose voices have been silenced. I have found that being present in court does make a difference. Judges are human; when the prosecutor informs the judge that the family of a victim is in court I believe this does serve to keep at least some attention on the victim, if only out of respect for the family, thus causing the victim to be seen as a person, rather than the inanimate object of the state's prosecutorial duty. Therefore, it is important to be present for as many court proceedings as possible. Along with this, keeping in frequent contact with the authorities, whether it's the police if an arrest has not been made, or the prosecutor's office if a suspect has been apprehended, really helps to keep the victim's voice active. Sitting back waiting for the authorities to contact you is foolish; they have enough to keep them busy, so unless you make it your business to speak for your loved one, the case can easily be moved to the back burner. Not that the justice system intends to forget or put off investigation of your victim's case, but you can be instrumental in keeping it in the public eye and keeping interest alive.

It is of utmost importance to continually support and advocate for victims' rights. In our current economic and political climate the cause of victims' rights has taken a back seat. Many crime victims' programs have lost funding; victims' rights are often forgotten among the most pressing issues of the day. Still, there is hope and there are movements to improve victims' rights. Search out legislators who have voting records that indicate their advocacy of victims' rights. Vote for them; help get them elected to office. Contact these legislators and make them aware that you are interested in what they are doing to advance the cause of victim's rights.

Among the rights that should be enacted is that of a family member to address the court during such proceedings as arraignment, guilty pleas, and appeals. As it now stands, the only opportunity we have to speak is via the Impact Statement at sentencing. If a family member of a victim tries to speak at any other than this designated time, he or she is escorted out of court. I have experienced where the father of my son's murderer has spoken in court, on two particular occasions, once when he tried to address the court regarding the unlikely event (according to him) of his son fleeing if his bail was reduced, and another time when he directly spoke to his son in court. He was not removed from court in those instances. However, we had been clearly warned prior to going into court that we were not permitted to speak.

Another right that would significantly improve the way the victim's family members are regarded would be to consider and consult the family before the decision is made to offer a plea. The time has come to stop excluding victims' families from this all important decision. My experience with this left me feeling powerless to speak for my son. We were told by the prosecutor when he spoke to us about their plans to offer a plea agreement to Jaire Highsmith, the murderer of my son, "We have an obligation to let you know what is happening, but the bottom line is, we drive the bus." Even though Highsmith had been indicted for first-degree murder, prosecutors would downgrade the charge to aggravated manslaughter and offer him thirty years rather than the life sentence he could get if found guilty of first degree murder in a jury trial. I argued with the prosecutor, telling him I did not agree that the charge should be downgraded to aggravated manslaughter. At the same time, I asked why the accomplice, Kenneth Walker, had not been charged. The prosecutor's reply: " We're not charging the accomplice; he's more use to us as a witness in case we need him." That was the end of his reply and at this point he was getting impatient with my questioning his authority. The prosecutor finally stated that they are in charge and we, in reality, didn't have any right to determine who, how or to what degree justice would be served for our son. Not having any say in these decisions is yet another slap in the face to family members of murder victims.

The American criminal justice system must have regard and respect for those who are closest to the reason for its existence; the victims and their families; people who loved them in life and have made a vow to ensure justice for them in death. The depth of feeling and grief does belong in court. Aside from what we've always been taught to believe, there is no sanitary, clean, unemotional homicide. A life has been taken in the most brutal manner, by a person who acted intentionally. This guilty person should experience at least the emotional pain he or she has inflicted upon the family of the victim. If our society were to clarify that this is the awful reality of murder, perhaps the homicide rate would decrease. As it is, we live in a world where many people have no idea of the horror murder wreaks upon all of those affected by it. Witness this through the prevalence of murder as entertainment venues: television, movies and even "Murder Mystery Dinner Theatres," used as fund-raisers. Much of our society envisions homicide as someone else's problem; something that will never touch them—until it does.

Stephen was a happy baby whose curiosity about the world led him to investigate how things worked. As he grew older, his fascination with electronics continued. He was an intelligent child, scoring in the 99th percentile in standardized tests. Frequent moves with the US Army made it difficult to put down roots with friends and extended family. As a result, Steve and Scott, his brother, who was seventeen months younger, were inseparable—where one went the other could also be found.

Jaire Highsmith, indicted for first-degree murder, pled to aggravated manslaughter—maximum of thirty years, 25.5 before eligibility for parole. What was his motive? According to him, Steve owed him money. Highsmith went to another acquaintance, Kenneth Walker, telling Walker that he was going to collect on this alleged debt. Walker instigated Highsmith, telling him he should go to Steve's apartment armed, then gave him a knife and rubber gloves. There is no premeditated murder in New Jersey.

My mind is racing. We haven't heard from Steve since Sunday. I can't get him on the phone; I have this ominous feeling and I'm afraid to go over there to check on him. I call him many times Monday, Tuesday, Wednesday. Finally, Thursday I call one last time. Then I call my daughter, Robin, and son-in-law, Brian, to check on Steve.

July 9, 2010. It has now been nearly nine years since Steve's murder. I've just heard from the appeals unit; Post Conviction Relief (PCR) denial is being appealed. It may be months or years before this one is heard. Constant upheaval. Never over. Just go away and serve your time. Stop trying to get out. If only you would admit what you have done. Not the short story; not the minimized, "cleaned-up" version. The whole awful crime you committed. Admit that you stabbed my son seventy-six times. That you nearly decapitated him. That you stabbed him in every vital organ of his body. You stabbed his head; you cut his throat. You did something so horrible that you are in denial. You have minimized it to make it sound less horrible to yourself, your family, and the court.

You don't care that we have to live with what you did to our child. We must contend with you constantly trying to get your sentence reduced, just anything you can possibly dream up to get a day out of prison to show up in court; ultimately, you hope it will get you a reduced sentence. Why don't you fade away and never be heard from again? The state is as guilty as you are for allowing this farce. Appeal after appeal—why are criminals allowed unlimited appeals?

November 9, 2001: Arraignment just finished; prosecutor advises us, "You are now long-distance runners in a marathon." That's exactly what this is—a hellish marathon. How long can we hold on? Who will outlive the other?

Who will be there for status conferences, guilty plea/plea bargains, sentencing, appeal, resentencing, appeal, post conviction relief motion, appeal… Who will be my son's voice?

Stephen Ronald Goebel, thirty years old, stabbed seventy-six times. My son can no longer speak for himself. His rights were taken away the night the murderer, Jaire Highsmith, stabbed him to death. The night the accomplice, Kenneth Walker, instigated the killer, gave him a knife and rubber gloves to go to Steve's apartment where he would try to extort money from Steve and then brutally kill him. Now I must speak for my son. As long as I live I will speak for him. I will be aware of every proceeding and I will be there. I want the judge to see me there, to know I am my son's voice, and to understand that my love for my child did not go to the grave with him.

# STEPHEN RONALD GOEBEL

## Born: January 29, 1971

### Victim of Homicide: October 29, 2001

November 1, 2001. "Mom, mom, it's Steve, he's dead…"
My son-in-law, Brian, hysterical, called me from Steve's
apartment. George had spoken to our son on Saturday.
He had asked Steve to come over on Sunday for dinner.
Life was overwhelming for Steve at that point. He had
lapsed into depression and emotional despair. He was
an easy mark—a victim…and there were plenty of
predators ready to pounce.

Steve had been an inpatient at Kennedy Hospital's
Crisis Unit on October 6th when I went to check on
the apartment. His patio door was shattered. I called
the police; they asked whether I had any idea who
might have done this. I told them there was a guy
called "Reds" in the next building. He had a pit bull
and was known to deal drugs. They did not question
Highsmith, a.k.a. "Reds." If he had been questioned,
would it have changed the outcome? Would he have
been arrested? Would we be going through this horror
now? Unanswered questions.

When Steve was released from the hospital the following week with medications and arrangements to be picked up daily for outpatient care, I was there. As I pulled up outside the apartment, the outpatient van was dropping Steve off in front of his apartment. At the same time, Kenny Walker came down the street toward us, holding a bag full of beer. When he saw me, he stopped. I said to Steve, "Don't get caught up in this. He doesn't care about you; he only wants a place to drink."

"Don't worry, Mom, I'll be all right."

Remember the marathon the prosecutor mentioned? That is fairly accurate. It's the longest race you will ever run. It never ends. After arraignment, there are numerous status conferences, attempts at plea deals, a plea or trial. If the murderer accepts the plea deal, there is the guilty plea followed by sentencing. At sentencing the criminal is told he must appeal within forty-five days. This is a cruel joke on the victim's family. In reality, at least in New Jersey, the murderer can use any flimsy "justification" to appeal his sentence. Then there is the instance where a case, disputing whether a fair sentence was handed down, is upheld by the state Supreme Court. All cases sentenced within a certain period of time are reviewed and resentenced to make sure the sentence is "fair." All the while you are asking yourself what is fair about the murderer sentencing your loved one to death. Resentencing accomplished, the appeal can now be returned to appellate court. If the appeal is turned down, the defendant has recourse to appeal to the Supreme Court. If the court is not buying it, just give it a little more time, then file a motion for Post-Conviction Relief. After all, doesn't the fact that the murderer was high on drugs or alcohol give him an excuse? Or, according to him, maybe his attorney didn't do all he could have to get a better plea deal. Better yet, he claims he didn't fully understand that he'd have five years probation after his sentence...even though at sentencing the judge asked point blank whether he understood everything that was said, and he replied that he did. When the judge hearing the PCR turns it down flat, it next goes to appellate court, at the state level. Do you sense a recursive process here...a never-ending, vicious cycle? Continuous assaults on survivors of homicide victims take their emotional toll and take the focus away from the victim. So you see why I must be my son's voice.

The night of October 29, 2001, our daughter, Robin, and son-in-law, Brian, left Steve's apartment around 9:30 p.m. He walked to the car with them, saying good night to his three-year-old niece, Alissa. At the same time, the predator was at the apartment of the accomplice, Walker, complaining that he needed money and was going to get some from Steve. Walker made it clear to Highsmith that Steve would not be an easy mark and he should be prepared for a fight. The accomplice gave him a large kitchen knife and a pair of rubber gloves. Highsmith walked to Steve's apartment, a distance of about two blocks from Walker's apartment. The lock on Steve's front door was loose and hadn't yet been repaired by the management. There were signs of forced entry as the wood molding around the area of the lock was splintered and the chain on the lock was broken.

What happened next has been the content of my nightmares for almost ten years. Steve's neighbor stated that she heard a series of loud thuds sometime between 9:30 and 11:00 p.m. She did not call the police. Steve had defensive wounds on his hands; he did not have a weapon. I can see him trying to fend off the blows of fists and knife from an assailant who was five inches taller and sixty pounds heavier than he was. According to the information I received from the medical examiner, Steve was most likely stabbed in his lungs first, making breathing or speaking impossible. By the time this brutal attack was finished, Steve had been stabbed seventy-six times: every vital organ pierced, his throat cut, and numerous wounds over his head and body.

This happened on Monday night. Kenneth Walker knew what had happened; he had helped to orchestrate this horror. He knew that Steve was dead. This information was covered in the interrogation. When Brian arrived at Steve's apartment on Thursday night, Walker nervously accompanied him. They went to the front door of the apartment. When there was no answer to Brian's knocks, he started to walk around to the back of the building. Walker stopped him, saying, "That's not a good idea." Brian continued around to the patio door. He noticed the door open about three inches. The television was still on. Brian went in and saw Steve's body lying on the floor face down, soaked in blood, as was the surrounding area. Brian called the Gloucester Twp. Police. Then he called us. We were in shock from the time I answered the phone. How we even drove to Steve's apartment was only through the grace of God.

When we arrived, numerous officers and detectives were already investigating. They had cordoned off the area around the apartment. Robin, Brian, and Kenneth Walker were in separate police cars, all waiting to be questioned. We were not allowed near the apartment. Meanwhile, Steve's body lay on the floor of the apartment as his murder was investigated and blood spatter samples were taken. His body was not removed until after midnight. Residents of the complex milled around outside that awful night. But one was conspicuously missing: Highsmith, a.k.a. "Reds."

Steve's body was taken to the Camden County Medical Examiner's Office. He was released to us on Saturday, November 3. I called the ME in desperation for answers. I needed to know how long Steve had suffered before dying of his wounds. The ME, obviously looking at this as just another job, told me with a nervous laugh that he had no way of knowing since some murderers can torture their victims for hours with stab wounds, while other victims die quicker, depending on the location and severity of the wounds. This was no help to me; in fact, it seemed cruel, as I had visions of my son suffering mercilessly. This is one of the reasons

I eventually consulted a credible psychic medium. I had to know all I could in order to deal with the reality of this horror. Otherwise I would never be able to put my visions to rest.

Most noticeable to us when Steve's apartment was released was that a large section of the carpet where his body had lain was cut out and taken as evidence. Blood was spattered on the walls and tape was placed at various places. Fingerprint powder was on furniture and walls.

As I write this, I am removed from it; as if I am speaking of a situation in which I have no stake. It is the only way I can complete this writing.

We gathered Steve's suit and good shoes to have him buried in. Why we were worried about his clothing is something I've never sorted out. It was obvious there would be a closed casket. Getting to the funeral home for arrangements took a major effort. I suppose in trying to blunt the effect of having a closed casket, we chose the most beautiful (if that is a way one can describe a casket) one available. There was a bronze relief of the Pieta on each corner. Somehow, I saw this as a way of relating to Jesus and His mother, Mary, and her suffering at His murder. It was a desperate effort to find a bit of comfort in the midst of wrenching pain. We would see our son one last time before closing the casket prior to the visitation. The funeral director did his best to make Steve's face somewhat presentable, but I'll never forget the way he looked; though I needed to see him, what had been done to him will always be indelibly burned into my memory.

Unknown to us, another assault was taking place while we buried our son. The management of the apartment complex had given orders to clear Steve's apartment out. We were not notified of this action even though the manager had access to all of our contact information in the office. Every piece of furniture, clothing, personal belongings, all that was left of our son, was hauled to dumpsters around the complex. This was discovered when Robin and Brian went to the apartment to place flowers at the door. The workers were inside tearing out the last of Steve's belongings to dump them. Police were called. The day of our son's funeral we were removing all that we could find from the dumpsters. What was the management's reasoning? They said they did it for health reasons. They had all of my information as next of kin. Addresses, phone numbers, everything. They never tried to contact us. This was Tuesday, November 6th.

During this time, Highsmith had been brought in for questioning. He failed a polygraph. He failed a voice test. He finally confessed and was arrested for the murder of our son. He was arraigned on Friday, November 9th. The coming months would bring status conferences, indictment, plea offers, guilty plea, and sentencing. In March 2002, the grand jury convened and indicted him for murder in the first degree. That sounds impressive, but don't let it fool you. The prosecutors decided the best plan was to downgrade to aggravated manslaughter, which carries a lesser sentence than murder. In fact, even though he had stabbed Steve seventy-six times, and obviously stabbing is an up-close and personal crime, the most the judge could sentence Highsmith to was thirty years/85 percent before parole eligibility. He will be considered for parole in 2027.

Plea offers help to clear the docket more quickly and, according to the prosecutors, they insure there will be a punishment, some sort of justice, rather than depending on a jury to convict the murderer. It took Highsmith some time to agree to the plea offer (notice that the murderer gets all the rights). Finally, his attorney convinced him he would be better off pleading guilty to aggravated manslaughter than taking his chances being tried for first-degree murder.

> *Guilty plea: the murderer's opportunity to minimize the crime in an effort to make it sound less horrendous than it actually is. When asked by the judge to explain the crime he had committed, he admitted to stabbing Steve one time. I was ready to jump over the barrier in the courtroom. Of course, I didn't because I knew I would be removed if I made any such attempt. Emotional displays are not permitted in the courtroom; actually, any attempt to speak can have one removed immediately.*

Between the plea and sentencing we focused on our impact statements. This is the only time the victim's voice can be heard in the courtroom. One may think that the prosecutor speaks for the victim; however, that is not true. The prosecutor speaks on behalf of the state. Laws must be upheld; when they are broken, the state must punish those responsible in order to help insure the continuation of a civil society. The impact statement becomes, for survivors of murder victims, the single most crucial document they will ever create. It is an extremely important way to be your loved one's voice, to break the silence that the murderer has imposed on the victim. Careful consideration is put into that statement and heartrending emotional upheaval is inherent in the crafting of the impact statement. I pondered how my statement would affect the judicial process responsible for sentencing my son's murderer. Moreover, I wanted it to have an impression on the killer. I had only this one chance to make it count. I took Steve's picture with me: a framed 8x10 that Highsmith couldn't miss as it sat turned toward him. Each of us gave our statement in turn, each faced with the same dilemma: How do you put a lifetime of love and a life sentence of grief into a brief statement? I posed this question to Joe, our grief counselor. He advised me to let the words flow from my heart.

> When you killed my son, you killed part of me. You killed a son, brother, grandson, nephew, uncle, cousin, friend. Many times, each and every day, the horrifying images bombard my consciousness. I stop whatever I am doing and try to compose myself, at home or at work— wherever I am. The images of my son being viciously stabbed over and over again won't go

away. The only relief is to pray for peace and try to sleep. God is good, He hears my cries and sees my tears; He brings angels in the form of friends to help. But I will never see my son as he was—my first born, sweet child, who would sit and have a cup of tea with me. Who would watch the *Honeymooners* reruns with me, who would write a poem for me, who would tell others how much he loved his family, who was deeply lonely and sad—prey for a murderer. I love him so; I miss him beyond words; I can't bring him back; you took his life. You stabbed him seventy-six times. Every time I think of this unspeakable horror, I feel every stab wound. How dare you admit to stabbing Stephen once—the coroner's report details the location, length, depth, and shape of each and every wound. How dare you take my child's life and leave me in such despair? We are empty shells since Steve's murder—his father and I, his brother and sisters—as if our hearts have been torn out of us. How dare you take my child's life? Your Honor, Jaire Highsmith has murdered my son. He has pled guilty to aggravated manslaughter, even though he was indicted for murder. I ask you to sentence Jaire Highsmith to the maximum penalty under the law.

The accomplice, Kenneth Walker, continued to walk free, unaffected by the horror that he had helped to wreak upon us. The prosecutor had made it clear that he would not press charges against the accomplice. This was unacceptable to me and never far from my thoughts. How could I insure justice would be done for Stephen regarding the person who had instigated and aided his murder?

Over the next four years I sought the assistance of several senators in surrounding districts. They really weren't interested in what I had to say; in fact, the senator of my district did not even return my calls. However, I finally found an ally in Senator Fred Madden, who welcomed me to his office and listened while I explained what I felt needed to be done. I wanted him to introduce a bill that would make it a crime not to report a known homicide. Sen. Madden explained that if such a bill became law it probably would not be effective because those who have knowledge of a homicide often have involvement in it and would be hesitant to help the authorities; surely they would not report the homicide, thinking that they would be implicated. I understood this explanation though I was not happy about it.

The need to have the accomplice charged and brought to justice never left my mind. It dogged my thoughts over and over. There had to be a way; some way of making him pay for his responsibility for what had been done to my son.

In the summer of 2006, I wrote to the appropriate prosecutor, asking her to return my son's belongings, which had been taken as evidence. She replied, explaining that in homicide cases personal effects are not returned. In addition, she mentioned that there was an appeal in the process. This hit me like a ton of bricks. I had not been notified of an appeal. I called Jim Lynch, acting Camden County prosecutor at the time. He understood when I told him how upsetting it was to learn of an appeal only because I had written a letter at just the right time. While we were discussing that point, I brought up the issue of the accomplice having never been charged. I felt as though this was the chance I had been waiting for. By the time our conversation was finished, Mr. Lynch had agreed to take another look at the case and get back to me in a few weeks.

This was the impetus for charges against the accomplice, Kenneth Walker. Eventually, he was arrested and indicted on the charge of murder. That charge was reduced to count one: hindering apprehension or prosecution, and count two: possession of a weapon for an unlawful purpose. He was supposed to serve six years for these two charges. However, when all was said and done, Walker served about six months total in jail before being assigned to Intensive Supervision Probation for eighteen months. He now walks free.

Survivors of murdered loved ones must be vigilant in pursuing justice for those whose voices have been silenced. I knew all along that this accomplice must be charged and even though the charges on which he was finally sentenced were not much more than a concession, at least he hadn't completely walked away after instigating Highsmith and providing the weapon used to murder my son.

Update: August 15, 2011. The prosecutor of the appellate unit called today to inform me that the PCR appeal is in process and will likely take a while longer before it reaches Appellate Court in Trenton. My heart sank, once again, as it does every time I hear from the prosecutor's office. But I must know so that I can cope with the situation.

Patricia Goebel

# CHRISTOPHER ACOSTA

## Born: July 14, 1978

### Victim of Homicide: September 12, 1999

The night our lives changed forever—September 12, 1999. We lost our son to murder. His name is Christopher Acosta. Christopher attended a large house party. Some girls were hit on the head with a can of beer. The guys that hit these girls were gang members. When the girls started talking back to these guys, the gang members got angry and knocked one of the girls out. When that happened, a boyfriend of one of the girls came to her defense. This started a fight between the gang members and the girl's boyfriend.

One of the gang members was losing his fight to the boyfriend. The other one shot up into the air with a gun to stop the fighting. The shots fired into the air stopped, and that's when my son headed over to see whether it was one of his friends being beaten by these gang members.

Christopher walked toward them. At that time, the gang member that was being beaten took the gun from the guy shooting into the air, and as my son approached, he shot to his right, to his left, and then right into our son's chest. It severed his aorta and left lung.

One of the witnesses said Christopher put his hand up as an automatic defense and told the guy, "No, no," not to shoot, but he did anyway. The shooting of our son may have also been mistaken identity, as Christopher and the guy defending the girls had the same build, both had the same color T-shirt, both wore a cap, and both had a light mustache.

We just don't know why they shot our son. He was never in a gang or associated with any. We think our son was either going to defend his friend, or going to leave the party as he was headed toward his car, which was only about ten feet from where he was shot.

Our son had no trauma to his hands, face, or anywhere else to indicate he had been fighting. His autopsy showed no alcohol or drugs in his system. He was an innocent bystander. Christopher was to meet a girl there that he had been dating.

We weren't allowed to see our son at the hospital. A rookie police officer told us we couldn't see him because it was a homicide. We didn't push it; we were in shock, and we didn't see Christopher until he was at the mortuary in St. Johns. He didn't even look like himself. They should have let us see him because it was our victim's right; however, we didn't know that at the time. I can't believe we let them do this to us. Our last good-bye didn't happen, and after the autopsy he didn't look like himself at all.

Another thing that really bothers me is that we were sent his autopsy photos in the mail. We thought we were ready for them after six years, and we let the prosecutor's office know that we wanted to see them. They had told us that when the time came that we would be able to go to their office with someone at our side to view the pictures. Instead, they sent the pictures to us in the mail, which was so traumatizing to us.

Christopher was a very responsible young man who had worked for a credit card company during his sophomore year of high school until he graduated, then he was hired full time. He saved his money and had just bought a new 1999 Firebird. He had enrolled at a junior college for the coming fall.

Our son would do anything for anyone, including his friends, which may have cost him his life. He loved his family, especially his five nieces and nephews. He would buy them the nicest and noisiest toys. He loved to watch them play and have a good time. Christopher would buy Christmas presents for his entire family and would go to any expense to give us what we would wish for Christmas. He would sit and watch us open our gifts just to see our expressions of pleasure. That look and smile we will never forget.

Chris was an altar boy from the time he was eight years old. He prayed all the time and attended Mass. He was a godfather to one of his nieces. She loved her uncle Christopher, and so did his other nieces and nephews. As a young child he loved to play pranks on us. He had such a big heart—his family meant everything to him.

We miss him terribly; he was our last child at home. He looked forward to marrying and raising a family.

Christopher's case has never been solved; it has become a cold case. He had just turned twenty-one years old when he was murdered. He had just begun his life. He wanted to be around his friends, and that is why he would attend these parties. We were always against it, but he said his friends went there to mingle and to meet girls. He would never understand that we worried about him going there.

Even though Christopher's case had been publicized in the media, no one came forward to say who did this to our son. They were scared, I suppose, and were friends to these gang members, so they did not speak up. No one seemed to care; a life didn't matter to any of these guys. His friends, too, seemed to not have seen anything, as everyone ran for cover when the shooting started.

As far as we are concerned, the detective who investigated Christopher's case did not do his job. He told my husband, "When it is a gang member shooting, we don't investigate that thoroughly because it is one less gang member on the streets." As he investigated, he found out that our son was a good, honest, and clean-cut young man who did all the right things. Except, of course, attend these no-good parties. These guys had gotten rid of the gun and got away with our son's murder. The detective did not interview these guys until two weeks after the murder. Out of more than a hundred kids at that party, he interviewed thirty-two kids, and most of those were our son's close friends. Those people were interviewed only because Christopher's brothers took them to the detective, not because he went out of his way to investigate.

The rest, to this day, stays the same. We doubt that we will see justice. It has been too long. When we went to the detective's supervisor to complain about the incompetent investigation into our son's murder, we were treated badly. They blackballed us and we had no calls or any answers whatsoever.

We are a family of one daughter and four boys. Christopher was the baby. He'd hate for you to say baby; let's say, the youngest. We had always been very close and have so many good memories. We all miss him. There is always that one person missing when there are family functions.

Christopher lives in our hearts forever. We feel he is always watching over our grandkids and the rest of his family. There is not one minute of all the hours of the day that we don't think of our son. Until the day we meet again, we look forward to seeing him.

Nora Acosta

# SHANE HEBERT

## Born: December 3, 1977

### Victim of Homicide: October 27, 1997

Where do I start to tell my story…December 3, 1977, when I gave birth to my first child, a son named Shane? Or October 27, 1997, when a gunshot took that same son away from me—both dates changed my life forever…

Shane was my firstborn and only son. He taught me so much about life even though he was the child and I the adult. Two daughters followed after him. He was a wonderful big brother and was very protective of his sisters. He was a caring son, father, husband, grandson, cousin, and friend. He meant so much to so many.

In April of 1997, my life seemed wonderful and so perfect. I thought I had it all. I became a grandmother for the first time with the birth of Shane's twin daughters Krista and Kristen. The next few months were some of the best and some of the busiest of our lives. Shane, his wife Tabitha, and the twins lived with us. We had a full house with them, my husband, our two daughters—Jennie and Laurie—and me. After a few months, we bought them a trailer and put it in our yard. Shane was so proud of his little family and his home.

Like I said, life was wonderful until the night of October 27, 1997, when my mother and Tabitha ran into my house screaming that Shane had been shot and was dead. My first reaction was anger at them for telling me something like that; there was no way it was true. He might be hurt, but not dead. Things like that happened to other people and on TV. Besides, if he was dead, I would *feel* it, and I didn't.

We rushed to the park where they said he was. I saw lots of people, police cars, and ambulances. I ran for the ambulance, knowing I would find Shane there—hurt but okay. It was empty... I saw policemen and paramedics by Shane's friend's car and tried to go to it, but I was held back by a police officer. I asked if my son was in the car and he said yes but would not let me go to him. I begged the paramedics to help him. They just looked at me with a helpless look on their faces and turned away. Later, I would understand the reason for this look. Finally, I saw our sheriff, who is also my cousin, talking to my brother. I asked him whether Shane was in that car. He said yes. I asked if he was dead; he took my hands and told me, "Yes..." Everything went black and I thought I was dying because I knew I surely could not survive losing one of my children. But I had only passed out. I was brought back, only to find out I was still alive and living a mother's worst nightmare. My son was gone.

The killers were found and arrested within a few hours of Shane's death. We found out that it was an armed robbery gone bad. Shane was not the intended victim. He had ridden to the ballpark with a friend. While they were sitting in the car talking to a boy standing outside of the car, a second boy ran up to the passenger side. He stuck a shotgun into the window. Shane's friend tried to take off; this pushed the gun into Shane's face and then the shooter pulled the trigger. Shane died instantly; he never saw the gun. The killer shot two more times at the car, hitting it and trying to kill the driver as he drove away. A third boy was involved. He remained in the car. We later found out that the boys intended to rob Shane's friend. They had no idea Shane would be in the car. Shane died at the park where he had played ball since he was five years old.

The next few weeks were a blur. I remember planning my son's funeral, saying good-bye, touching him for the last time, giving him a last kiss on his forehead, running my fingers through his hair, and then burying him. It was all like a dream—a nightmare. Afterward, I would get up in the mornings, forgetting while I slept that my child was dead. I would have to face the reality of him being gone again each morning. I never knew a person could feel such pain and live through it. My life as I knew it was over; the person I once was, gone. My two daughters not only had lost their brother, but they had lost the mom they had always known. My husband was not only dealing with the loss of his son but with a wife who had fallen apart. I was terrified to let my daughters out of my sight; no longer were they allowed to go to their friends' houses or do anything I thought might be dangerous like riding bikes or go-carts. I lived in fear of losing another child.

Then, just as I would start to get better, as the shock would subside and I was able to function, we would have to go to court. In the two and a half years it took to finally go to trial, we were in court more than a dozen times, only to have it continued by request of the defense. Everything was focused on the killer's rights. I felt we had buried Shane's rights with him. Finally, in April of 2000, we went to trial. It was so hard to sit in the courtroom and look at the person who took my son's life, to hear the details of how he died, and have the defense dehumanize my son's life. He never once referred to my son by his name; he was always "that kid." I wanted to scream, "He has a name and it is *Shane*!" For three days I had to sit and hold my emotions in.

Then came the verdict…not guilty. I was in shock and disbelief. How could this happen? I felt like I had lost Shane all over again. I have been told that after the verdict I stood up and started crying and screaming. My husband was allowed to take me from the courtroom. We had to go home and tell our daughters that the person who killed their brother got away with it and would not be punished. Later that evening, we got a call from the district attorney's office. They informed us that after being taken back to the jail to be processed out, the killer had confessed to killing Shane, but said that it had been an accident. He walked up to the car with a loaded shotgun and his finger was on the trigger. After shooting Shane, he then shot two more times as the car was speeding away. This was an accident?

It was then that I learned what Double Jeopardy means. Once a person has been found not guilty of a crime, they can't be tried for that crime again. He killed Shane and was walking free. I lost all faith in the *justice system*. We had to have an alarm system installed in our home because our daughters lived in fear. Someone had killed their brother and he was free. He could come to our house and kill them or someone else they loved. The screams from their nightmares woke me many nights. I would sit and hold them as they cried and try to reassure them. I watched my son's two baby daughters be confused, not knowing where their daddy had gone. They were too young to understand, but knew a part of their world was missing.

The next few years were filled with hate and anger. I was so bitter and was letting it turn me into someone I did not like. I realized that not only had he taken Shane from my family, he had taken me too. I decided he had taken enough and would get no more from my family. I learned to deal with the anger and let it go. It wasn't always easy, but I knew to have any kind of life I could no longer allow this killer to have a hold on me.

Losing Shane has been the hardest thing I have ever had to deal with in my life. It has changed my life in every way and forever. At this time, it has been thirteen years since Shane was murdered. I am at a point where I enjoy life again and have learned to live with the pain. It has been the most difficult journey one could imagine. I have watched Shane's daughters grow up without their daddy. So much has been taken from them; they have been cheated—no father-daughter dances, no daddy to hug them when they skinned their knees or had their hearts broken, no daddy to walk them down the aisle when they get married. So much that should have been but now can never be. Shane would be in his thirties now, but I can't picture it; to me he is still nineteen and always will be.

I have learned that life is not always fair. I have found that people do not know how to deal with a person who has lost a child. I have lost friends on this journey; they kept waiting for me to get back to the "old me," not understanding that person is gone forever. I am a new person now. In some ways I am a better person than I was before; I have learned what is important in life and not to waste a moment of it. I will always hurt and miss my child. A part of me is gone forever—I can't change it—I can't fix it, so I have learned to live with it and try to be the best person I can be. I know it is what Shane would want me to do.

I started Angel Moms, an online grief support group, in January 2001, with the help of two other moms. Angel Moms began with twelve members and has grown to over 800 moms who have lost their children to a variety of causes. After Shane's murder and the trial, I was a member of a small group of moms who e-mailed privately. Other moms would hear about it and want to join, but some moms in the group wanted to keep it small and private. I felt badly for those who wanted to join because I knew how important it is to have support. I started Angel Moms so any mom who had lost a child could join. When I started the group, I never dreamed it would become what it has today.

Judi Walker

# TIMOTHY CLARK

## Born: December 31, 1991

### Victim of Homicide: July 13, 2007

My son, Timothy Patrick Clark, was brutally murdered on July 13, 2007. He was fifteen years old. My oldest son, Joey, had a friend, Damien, who had been staying with us off and on, as he was having trouble with his girlfriend and her family, whom he had been living with. I didn't mind because he was a nice guy. He did landscaping work around the neighborhood and took the younger guys with him to earn some money— pocket change—for the summer. Damien was at my house on Thursday, July 12th. I remember before going to bed that Timmy was on the computer. I rubbed his head; I can still feel his hair on my fingers. I said to him, "Don't stay up late," and he responded, "I won't; I'm tired"—his last words to me. I said, "Okay, good night baby cakes, love ya"—my last words to him.

I went to bed only to be awakened at 4:20 a.m. on Friday, July 13, 2007. My oldest son woke me up. He had another man with him—behind him. He was a neighbor. I thought this was odd. Joey said to me, "You have to come downstairs; something happened." So I went down and there was another man, a very big man in a suit. He started asking me all kinds of questions; my name, address, phone number…I kept thinking, *Oh my God, what did Joey do*, because he was just standing there, staring at me, and I couldn't figure out why this guy was asking me all of these questions. I finally sat there and said, "What is this all about; what is going on?" They just stared at me. Then, finally, my son (who, to this day, I believe should not have been the one to tell me, and you'll see why as this story progresses) said to me, "Timmy's dead."

I jumped up and started screaming, "What, what, what? No, there is a mistake; they have the wrong kid. Where are my shoes? Take me there. Where is he? You made a mistake." I kept running around the house looking for my shoes, saying this over and over again.

I finally found my shoes and bolted outside. Down the street from where I live, right at the corner, I could see all kinds of flashing lights and police cars. I headed down that way, when my son grabbed me and said, "No, you can't go down there."

I said, "Yes, I am, there is a mistake." Then I pulled away from him as the other two men grabbed me. They held me back; I fell to my knees, trying to force myself away from them. Then, what finally stopped me was my son. He said, "Please, Mom, don't go down there, please," and I knew right then what they told me was true. I didn't even realize the screams that followed were coming from me.

Timmy was shot in the back of his head. He died at the scene. Damien, who was twenty-six years old, was shot through the jaw, severing his spinal cord. He died two days later. Damien had been showing Timmy how to use the lawn mowing equipment after I went to bed. A friend of his stopped by and told me he was asleep on the sofa, and she woke him up. She still feels terrible about this, thinking that if she hadn't awakened him he'd still be alive. Damien, then, must have asked Timmy to walk with him to the corner store to buy snacks for that night and the next day. Timmy had no money and, of course, he'd go with Damien to get food. Timmy loved to eat; he was going to be a big boy!

At first, they didn't know who the young boy was, lying there. A friend of my oldest son came to our house and woke him up. He told my son there had been a shooting down the street and they thought it might be Timmy. When he went outside, a detective was standing there. He asked my son whether his father was home. My son told him, "No, he doesn't live here."

"Anyone older in the house?"

"My mother; she is sleeping."

He then asked my son to wake me, and my son said, "No, I will not let my mother go down there. I'll see if it is my brother." He is the one who identified his baby brother lying there on the pavement—a vision that causes him to have nightmares every night. This picture is burned inside his brain. It's an awful thing to live with at such a young age.

The detectives know Damien and Timmy went to the store and bought snacks; their bags were found still there on the street where they were dropped. They were not robbed. Damien still had money in his pocket. We could not figure out who could do this to them. It was a nightmare, burying my fifteen-year-old son—something no mother should ever have to do. I remember so much of those few days, and so little of the months following. I went numb. People asked me questions, I could hardly think straight. It was so hard, but we had a wonderful detective. He always answered my calls or my emails. Even as the months went by, he would still call me back or respond to my emails. I know how hard he worked on my son's case. This is something I will always remember. For our part, we raised reward money by holding Beef and Beers. Finally, after fourteen months, the police made an arrest.

In September 2008, I received a phone call from our detective. He asked whether he could stop by the house. When he arrived, he told me to sit down and proceeded to tell me that they had arrested two men, and they knew which one was the shooter. I started to cry. I found out that it was the brother and brother-in-law of Damien's girlfriend. They didn't like Damien because he was black. My Timmy was "a casualty of war"; he was in the wrong place at the wrong time.

The trial was awful, arduous, and just terribly draining on all of us. I don't know how many times people would say, " Now you have closure." No, we will never have closure. We have an ending to a chapter of this awful nightmare we live in. The media covered the trial very well. There were so many articles about the defendants and the proceedings. One of the defendant's brothers was arrested for witness intimidation. He had just been released from jail this past October. The two murderers were sentenced to double life without parole, plus thirty more years for other offenses. The one who actually shot Timmy and Damian escaped the death penalty by one juror. The jury deadlocked 11-1, which is okay with me. I hope they both close their eyes every night and see my baby's face. They showed no remorse during the trial and sentencing.

Throughout the trial, the detective, officers of the court, judge, and jury—twelve people who saw through the callousness of these two evil men—were wonderful. Everyone was helpful, fair, and caring. The assistant district attorney was competent and assured. I would never want to be up against him—that is for sure.

Thinking about the trial pains me deeply. When people ask me about it I try to discuss it with them, and then I wind up asking them to check out the articles because there is a lot I don't remember, or maybe I have blocked out some of the most painful parts. We had many delays, then the holidays, and we were back in January for the penalty phase. All of this during December, which is my birthday; Christmas, which is my son Matt's birthday; then New Year's Eve, which is Timmy's birthday; and a trial in the middle of it all. It was surreal to say the least. To add to the nightmare was the reality of having to be not only in the same courtroom as the murderers' families, but to also be in the same waiting area while the jury was sequestered. I had lost my baby, my sweet Timmy, to the hateful hands of the killers; now I felt I was losing my mind. However, I was committed to being my son's voice through it all.

I summoned every nerve in my body to read the impact statement, which I had so carefully prepared. Reading that statement was one of the hardest things I ever had to do, but I did. I was his voice that day and there was not a dry eye in the courtroom, including my tough ADA, who cried right along with me.

> Timmy was a great kid. He was very shy, but he was making a lot of new friends. They always hung out at my house and I didn't mind so much; not to say I liked picking up after them! I remember all the times I would get on his case about them always being here; I regret that now. I miss the commotion and the noise! He loved playing football. He wanted to be a quarterback. His favorite team was the Pittsburgh Steelers, and I would often buy him different caps for the team. He had a great sense of humor and had the best belly laugh ever! He had the kind of laugh, that when he laughed, even at the slightest thing, everyone would laugh with him. He was just that type of person. My Timmy had the brightest, big blue eyes and a goofy grin with big dimples.

Like most teenagers, my son loved playing Xbox and PlayStation 2. His favorite games were *Oblivion* and *Final Fantasy VII*. He enjoyed drawing and was very artistically talented. He never bothered anyone; he was a good person, a kind soul. Timmy always helped our neighbors, even turning down the offer of money for helping with grocery bags or helping with some kind of chore. He loved animals and always brought home strays. My house was constantly filled with friends and different kinds of animals, from fish and hamsters to guinea pigs, cats, or dogs. He couldn't stand to see an animal scared or being neglected. The best way to describe him is, as I said before; he was a kind soul, always there for his friends, no matter what. If anyone needed him or just wanted someone to talk to, Timmy was always available. He also was my youngest son, my buddy. We would go everywhere together; sometimes he would just go to the store with me so that he could listen to the radio and ride with me in the car. He always greeted me when I came home from work. If he and his friends were outside playing football or basketball, he would stop and wait for me to park, then walk over to the car to ask how my day was.

[Now I have to stop because I'm crying.]

I have never before felt such pain as I have now, losing my son this way. This pain is deep and never-ending. It's within my heart and soul; a piece of me has been taken away, never to be returned. I will never feel whole again. My life will never be the same; I am a different person. I am torn apart; my family has been torn apart. Timmy's brothers will endure this pain for a lifetime. To be so young and going through this kind of pain is unthinkable. Most people don't understand the pain of losing a child, especially to murder. I've lost many friends, many people who, I guess, cannot understand and maybe feel uncomfortable being around me. However, our pain lasts a lifetime, and I've met many wonderful people on this awful journey, and I do believe that God puts certain people in your life for a reason. It is not a group I would want to welcome anyone into, but I am very grateful to know people who share my grief and pain and understand what I'm going through.

Timmy's two brothers have endured so much pain in their lives. His oldest brother has nightmares from having to identify him. He not only lost his baby brother; he lost a friend as well. His other brother would let Timmy hang out with him sometimes. It made Timmy feel so great to hang out with his older brother and his friends. Some days they can't even talk about it, and then some days the memories shine through, but I know that in their hearts they realize this is all they have left—the memories.

It has taken me a long time to think of a way to finish Timmy's story, but then I realized that there really is no ending. My son is gone; he was taken away from me, his loving family, his friends, and neighbors, through evil that overtook someone's heart. Our pain will live on forever; my son's memories will live on forever; my love for my son, Timothy Patrick Clark, will live on forever. As long as I breathe I will be here to tell his story. There will be no end, as love never dies.

Bette Ann Clark

# ROBERT UCCIFERRI

## Born: October 20, 1961

### Victim of Homicide: March 30, 2002

Bobby Ucciferri's voice was silenced on March 30, 2002. Bobby, forty years old, was shot twice in the head. He had gone to the American Legion Post 372 in Cherry Hill, New Jersey, on Friday evening, March 29th. Although not a member, he was a familiar face at the Legion, but not a drinker. The Commander said that Bobby only drank coke when he was there.

Bobby was last seen alive on Saturday at 2:30 a.m. as he left the post with a man and woman acquaintance who lived three houses from Bobby's former wife and their children. Bobby had told his brother Louis that this man had approached him while he was working across the street from where Bobby's family lived. Bobby had found out that his ex-wife had borrowed $2800 from the acquaintance's mother, and he demanded that Bobby pay it back. Bobby had known nothing of the loan prior to this, but he did know of this man's background and his recent release from prison after serving sixteen years for armed robbery. Bobby reached in his pocket and gave the guy three hundred dollars. He took the money and demanded the balance be paid immediately.

The morning of March 30, 2002, the post had an Easter egg hunt on the same grounds where Bobby's truck sat with the dome light on. This was noticed by an employee of the post at that time, but no one checked to see if anyone was in the truck. That night, the same employee noticed the truck was still there with the dome light still on and had someone go with her to see why the truck was still there. They found Bobby slumped over the steering wheel with two bullets in his head.

Bobby was born on October 20, 1961. He was one of seven children born to us. He was our first son. He had three sisters and three brothers. One sister, Kathy, was older; and Michael, Stephen, Donna, Lynnette, and Louis were younger. Bobby attended Queen of Heaven Grammar School and Cherry Hill West High School, which happens to be located in front of the American Legion Hall. Bobby served four years in the US Navy. After he was discharged from military service, he worked in construction, building houses and additions. He also opened a stone yard in Cherry Hill. He was quite talented in many areas.

In 1987, Bobby married. Four children were born of this marriage: Angela, Kristina, Robert, and Anthony. Bobby was devoted to his children, as well as to his wife's son, who was eleven months old when

Bobby met her. He raised the boy as his own son. The marriage ended in 1999.

It was Easter weekend; my husband, Bob, and I were going to the Poconos to spend the holiday with our daughter, Kathy, and her family. I had talked to Bobby before we left and he said, "I guess I'll spend Easter alone since I have to work this weekend." Our son Louis and daughter-in-law Shayni surprised us by making the trip to the Poconos that weekend. It was a pleasure to have two of our children's families with us, and on Easter morning we all went to Mass together. When we returned from church, Louis had a message from his neighbor that Cherry Hill Police were at his door at about 11 p.m. Saturday night. John, our daughter Kathy's husband, also had a message to call our son Michael.

Michael had received a call from his Aunt Helen that Bobby had been found shot at the American Legion. They had tried to reach us, and then our son Louis. The terror of the moment when John returned Michael's call is something we will never forget. We had Bobby's oldest daughter, Angela, with us. How do you tell a fifteen-year-old that her father was found shot to death?

The trip home was a nightmare. When we arrived, our children—Michael, Stephen, Donna, and Lynnette—were at our house with other relatives. Kathy and John also traveled from the Poconos with their family. This was a bad dream that we wanted to wake up from. The next few days were a fog. Bob and our sons went to identify Bobby the next morning, while the officials from the prosecutor's office were at our home, trying to get as much information as possible. We had no idea why this happened and who was responsible. No weapon was ever found.

On Monday, our daughter Lynnette and her husband, Nick, went with us to make arrangements for the funeral. The funeral was very emotional for our family and friends. Several hundred people attended. Bobby was well liked; he had grown up in this township. He had grown up around the corner from the American Legion.

Time went on and the prosecutor's office and the Cherry Hill Police questioned dozens of people many times. After awhile, with no one coming forward, our family offered a reward. More information and leads were coming in. Many of the same people were questioned again. Some of these leads have taken our Cherry Hill detectives as far as Florida. So far, because of a lack of evidence, an arrest has not been made.

Nine years have passed; Bobby's murder has become a cold case. Occasionally we hear from the prosecutor's office. The victim-witness advocate will call on the anniversary of our son's death; otherwise, all is quiet. The years have been rough on Bobby's children. Angela and Kristina quit school to help support the family. Their home life has been far from perfect. Angela finally went to live in the Poconos with our daughter Kathy's family. She earned her high school diploma and is now in her third year of college, working full time and doing well. She has resided with Kathy for four years and has made a new life for herself. Kristina is doing well and is the mother of a baby boy—Bobby's first grandchild. Robert and Anthony went to live with our son Louis and his family, after the court awarded them custody four years ago. Robert is now on his own and attending community college. Anthony has been legally adopted by Louis and Shayni as of December 2009. He attends private school with his cousins. Bobby had spent many weekends at Louis and Shayni's with Anthony, his youngest son, after his divorce.

We attended counseling with Survivors of Traumatic Grief and still meet with our grief counselor occasionally. We know we could not have dealt with this without the support of our family, friends, and God. We hope that God will someday grant our family peace, and justice for Bobby. Until that time, we will speak for Bobby; we will be his voice.

Madeline Ucciferri

# RACHEL DENNIS

## Born: February 26, 1984
### Victim of Homicide: March 2, 2007

March 3, 2007, started out to be a fun day. I was shopping with my daughter Rebecca. When we returned from shopping, Rebecca's boyfriend, Tim, notified us that my daughter Rachel was missing. He had received a call from her father, who lived in Coffeyville, Kansas. Apparently, Rachel had called her roommate around 8:30 p.m. on the night of March 1st to check on her son, Tegan. She said she would be home soon. We knew she would never leave Tegan, who was twenty-one months of age. While Rebecca and Tim tried to reassure me that she could be off somewhere recovering from a binge of some sort, we all knew something was desperately wrong. This was the day that my life changed forever.

All I have left of my daughter is an urn with her ashes and a few of her personal belongings. Of course, I have a file full of newspaper clippings and hearing and trial notes, but I really can't bear to look at that file unless I need information from it. Since her murderer has filed an automatic appeal, I fear I will have to review that file and sit through more hearings in the future. I don't think a conviction of capital murder is ever final due to the "rights" of the murderers to file appeals. Nor does a conviction ever bring "closure" to a family. What closure? I have to continue this life without her. He received life without the possibility of parole and was convicted of capital murder, but somehow this sentence doesn't seem equal to taking my Rachel from her family. The attorney general's office made the decision not to go after the death penalty. I recognized that his death would not bring Rachel back, and I wanted him to live long and suffer, accordingly, by remembering and reliving what he did to my daughter.

The name of this monster who murdered my daughter is Christopher Lawrence of Coffeyville, Kansas. My daughter knew him only through other friends she had made contact with upon returning to Kansas with her son. She had decided to move to Kansas just ten months prior to her death to raise Tegan in the same area in which she was raised. We had argued the last night she and Tegan lived in our home. She was angry and said she was taking him back to Kansas, which is where her father still lived. She packed and drove out of my driveway that same night. Oh, how I wish I had stopped her from leaving. So many things that we had fought about that night are trivial when comparing them to not having her anymore. There are so many what ifs…

Rachel had just turned twenty-six years old on February 26th. She went missing March 1st and it was later discovered that she was murdered on March 2nd. On March 1st Rachel left Tegan with her roommate, telling her that she would be back after picking up some film at Wal-Mart. A friend, Shelly, was taking her. While at Wal-Mart, Rachel and Shelly ran into acquaintances, and an instant "party" was created. Rachel called the roommate at 8:30  p.m., telling her she had gone to Shelly's house for a party. It was a Thursday night. By Friday night, Laura, Rachel's roommate, realized something was wrong and called Rachel's father and stepmother. They came and picked up Tegan and some things he would need to stay with them until Rachel came home, which, of course, never happened. I was notified Saturday afternoon that my daughter was missing. No one called me; my daughter Rebecca's boyfriend told me and filled me in on what details were known. A sick feeling in my body told me that this was not Rachel just being immature and careless, even though I wanted to believe that was all it was. Her father notified the police.

Worse than knowing my daughter was no longer alive was that she was missing for thirteen days. I was in Phoenix, Arizona, and she was missing from Coffeyville, Kansas. My life stopped. I didn't know whether I should go out there or just stay by the phone. Rachel's stepmother talked to me on the phone, telling me that there was nothing I could do if I did come, and to wait until they knew what was going on. I waited by the phone, calling and waiting for calls, to know what was happening with the search. I hadn't heard from the detectives assigned to Rachel's case so I called them. I wanted them to know Rebecca and I needed to be informed of all information they were obtaining. I was assured I would be called with all new information. Mainly, it turned out to be me making the effort to stay in touch with the Coffeyville police and insisting on information.

I had raised Rachel and Rebecca as a single parent and had always considered the three of us as a single unit. We had a saying in our household: "Together forever." I had given Rachel a locket with those words engraved on the back of it and Rebecca's and my pictures inside. It was to be a comfort to her when she and her sister went on court-mandated, weekend visitation with their father. I knew those words were important, but I didn't fully realize the significance of them until I had to cling to those words in the hopes that we would be together again. Now, because Rebecca and I were living in another state, it was as if we didn't matter. I knew Rachel better than anyone and I was the one having to contact the detectives to tell them of Rachel's personality. They asked if I thought she would leave her son to go with friends for this length of time. Rachel had her faults and was immature at times, but there was no way she would willingly leave her family for this long.

The day the detective said he might need my DNA, my mind told me Rachel was gone, but my heart insisted there was a possibility she was sick or being held against her will. Blood had been found in someone's vehicle. Still, there was hope in my heart, even as I lay on my bed crying and repeating, "Rachel, what have you done?" Yes, I was angry with her, but later I learned that that was a normal reaction, whatever normal is, to such devastating news.

I knew it was raining in Coffeyville and kept thinking of my daughter being in the woods somewhere, cold and wet and needing help. While volunteers searched, newspapers and TV media covered the case. Everyone in that small town wanted to know what had happened to the beautiful young mother. Residents in rural areas were asked to search their properties and buildings, but still no trace of Rachel was found. The last people she was known to be with were interviewed and, of course, no one knew what happened. Information was being pieced together. Rachel had been at Shelly's house, and then she was asked to leave. Some of the partygoers moved to another person's house to continue the party. Rachel was one of those who chose to continue partying. Rachel was drinking heavily and passed out on a sofa at that house, which was only two blocks from where she lived with Tegan and Laura. Christopher offered to take her home, but others said to let her sleep it off. She could go home in the morning. Christopher insisted that he take her the two blocks to her house and would make sure she got home safely. He ran three blocks to his house to get the car that his wife and child had used when they left the party earlier.

They were already in bed and never knew that he had taken the car. If only his wife had been awake to stop her husband from what he was about to do.

After arriving back at the house with his car, he convinced two other men to carry Rachel to his vehicle and put her inside. They even had to carry her purse. Rachel had no idea what was happening or going to happen to her. She just wanted to sleep. He drove three miles (remember that she was only two blocks from her house to the party) to a convenience store where she was spotted in his vehicle with her head leaning against the window, but she was still alive. This was around 6 a.m. Friday. By 6:30 a.m. my daughter had been taken from this earth. Thirteen days later, Christopher would take the authorities to my daughter's body—her remains.

During the trial, he said he did not kill her, but looked over and saw that she was already dead and panicked. Rachel revealed the truth. Her body told the story. She had been beaten, causing internal injuries; hit on the head, causing an open head wound; raped or attempted rape (unable to be determined due to the length of time in the water); strangled with her own cell phone cord from the phone she had just received for her birthday; and then thrown off a bridge into dark, murky waters.

As I stood on that bridge to see where my daughter had been thrown from, I saw a bedspring and other trash floating in the water. I will never forget that moment of realizing that monster had thrown my flesh and blood away with the trash. This was only learned through investigation and what came out at trial. He couldn't even leave her where she died.

The day that Rachel died, my faith died. I can't understand why God didn't save her or at least let her pass with more dignity and not have to endure such suffering. I couldn't protect her or tell her I loved her. All she wanted in her life was to love and to have someone love her in that same way. I still can't pray or talk about God. In a way, I suppose I blame Him for not protecting my daughter. I used to believe that God is love, but I honestly don't know what I believe anymore. I want to believe in everlasting life and love, but the truth is that I can't say that I do anymore. Meanwhile, life goes on.

The days after her death had been confirmed, my body functions shut down. I couldn't talk in a normal tone or speed. I had to pause between each word to think about the word I needed to say next. I couldn't drive for the first month and had to walk or ride a bike if I needed to go somewhere. I couldn't work. Nothing mattered. I had lost my daughter. Through time, I have recovered enough to continue living, enjoying my daughter Rebecca and the beautiful grandchildren both my daughters have given me. They are a gift and reason to push onward and to continue growing older each year—until the time comes that I can be reunited with Rachel in her world—wherever that is. I still have many questions and thoughts about what happened to my beautiful daughter.

Hopefully, talking about my sorrow can help ease someone else's sorrow. Her murderer received a life sentence, but her family did too—a life without Rachel. I always seem to have that empty chamber in my heart that is reserved for my taken child. It feels like she was ripped from my arms. In a strange way, it has been Rachel who has given me the strength to go back to school to complete my early childhood degree. She loved the four- and five-year-olds and worked as a day care teacher. Now I am working with the same age group in a Head Start classroom.

Our relationship wasn't always as close as I wanted, and I so wish I could have that time with her to explain that I lived my life for her and her sister and made the best decisions I could in raising them. Rachel was the entertainer in the family. She was in five musicals while elementary school age, tapped her way through several dance recitals, and always thought of activities to make weekends and holidays fun. We enjoyed musicals, especially *Phantom of the Opera*. I was in our neighborhood electronics store recently when a song from *Phantom* came on. It took me by surprise; it was all I could do to keep myself from falling apart. Even after almost four years, I have panic attacks over the reality of what has happened. It doesn't seem to matter though, nothing changes as I still wake up every day remembering she is gone—gone from this world—

gone from communicating with her son, her sister, and me. Together forever, Rachel.

Patti Howick

# JARRED NEAL

## Born: May 25, 1996

### Victim of Homicide: June 30, 1999

Jarred Neal was my grandson. He was three years old when his mother's boyfriend physically abused him and caused his death. His mother, Melanie, and father, Brian, were separated at the time; Brian lived out of state. Jarred's parents separated when he was approximately twenty-eight months old. Jarred and his older sister, Jade, remained in the custody of their mother. While working at a convenience store, Melanie met her boyfriend and allowed him to move in with her and the two children. Not long after, the boyfriend became angry with Jarred and was chasing him in order to punish him. Melanie stepped in between Brad, her boyfriend, and Jarred. Brad twisted Melanie's arm so hard that he broke it. It was two to three months after Brad moved in that Jarred was killed.

Some of the information of what occurred during that time is unclear. Various stories were told by Brad and Melanie, and what the police were able to piece together is partially speculation. It was a Friday when

Melanie had a friend take her to court to obtain an order of protection against Brad, to have him removed from the apartment. Melanie told the judge, in the sworn affidavit, that she feared for the lives of herself and her children if Brad remained at the residence. That evening, when Brad returned to the apartment, Melanie chose not to have the order of protection served to him. Melanie claimed that she, Brad, and the two children spent the weekend at home, and she hadn't left Brad alone with Jarred and Jade for more than five minutes at a time throughout the weekend. The police reports indicate that Jarred had been sick all weekend, vomiting and walking into walls and furniture. Jarred was still ill on Monday. Melanie went to work and Jade went to daycare, while Brad agreed to stay home with Jarred. This was the first time that Brad had ever watched Jarred while Melanie was at work. She normally took the children to a sick child daycare at a local hospital.

That same morning, a neighbor reported during the investigation that Brad was seen dragging Jarred from the car, through the bushes, and to the apartment. Unfortunately, Brad and Jarred and the apartment they entered, were not clearly identified so this report could not be used as evidence. Later that day, Brad claimed he put Jarred in the shower with him because Jarred had been vomiting and he wanted to clean him up. He said that Jarred had fallen a couple of times while in the shower and his head had hit the bathtub. His claim was that these falls accounted for the head injury later found on Jarred. Brad reported that after the shower, Jarred lay down on the bathroom floor because he was tired, so Brad left him there to rest. Later, he claimed that he wrapped Jarred in a towel and put him on the bed. He left Jarred on the bed while he went to pick up Melanie from work and Jade from daycare.

When Melanie arrived home, she looked at Jarred and called the doctor's office. She explained to the nurse that Jarred was breathing, but his eyes were partially open and he wasn't responding to her voice or touch. The nurse told her to take him to the emergency room. They took Jarred to an urgent care center where arrangements were immediately made to have Jarred flown to a pediatric hospital. Doctors contacted the police since Jarred's injuries were consistent with abuse. The police came to the hospital, along with Child Protective Services, to speak with Melanie and Brad. Melanie claimed, falsely, that there weren't any relatives in the state of Arizona who could care for Jade, so CPS took her into their custody at that time.

My husband David's ex-wife received a late night call the next day from Melanie's friend and boss at the convenience store, advising us that Jarred was hospitalized. At that particular time, the friend did not know the severity or reason for Jarred's hospitalization, just that Melanie had called out of work for that reason. Because of the lack of detailed information and lateness of the call, we were not made aware of Jarred's grave condition until the next morning. Jarred was hospitalized for approximately three days before he died. He was brain dead upon arrival, but he was kept on life support until his father could return to Arizona from out of state. After confirming that Jarred was in the hospital, was not expected to live, and that child abuse was suspected, my husband began making phone calls to determine where Jade was and what needed to be done to have her placed in our home.

At the time of Jarred's death, both my husband and I worked at the Glendale Police Department. This was helpful because we were aware of how the criminal justice system worked. The county attorney assigned to the case was excellent, as was the victim assistance caseworker.

The criminal justice process is often long and frustrating. Once every month the defendants are taken into court where the attorneys and the judge discuss whether they are ready to go to trial. These are status conferences. During the monthly court hearings, a discussion regarding the investigation process, as well as any motions being brought forth by either attorney, are heard by the judge to determine a ruling. The judge must also authorize a continuance of the incarceration of the defendants. Every month we would attend the hearings, hopeful that a trial date would be set, and were disappointed to find out that it wouldn't be. The state's attorney and the defense attorney would take time after the hearing to explain what had occurred and what to expect in the future. Oftentimes, the defense attorney would also stop to talk with us regarding the situation and assist with the explanations. Both attorneys would always ask about Jade's well-being and her progress with counseling. Anytime we had questions, we could contact the state's attorney or the victim assistance caseworker, who were always willing to listen and give us answers as best they could.

As a possible trial date approached, it was determined that Jade might have to testify during the trial. The victim assistance caseworker arranged for Jade to attend a Kids at Court session where they explained the entire process and provided a tour of the courtroom and judge's chambers. The caseworker spoke directly to Jade, being very compassionate and understanding of the circumstances and Jade's behavior, due to the traumatic situation she had witnessed.

The most frustrating part of the court process was the length of time involved, particularly for this type of case. It took almost three years before a final determination was made and sentencing occurred. There were times during the process that, as victims, we wondered whether the suspect's *rights* were more important than ours. We hadn't asked for this terrible situation, nor were we involved in creating it; we had lost our beloved, innocent, three-year-old grandson, the light of our lives, and now we were living through a three-year nightmare.

There were actually two cases pending, which added to the frustration. The boyfriend was indicted for murder and was potentially facing the death penalty. The mother was also charged because she had failed to protect both of her children—her son, Jarred, who was murdered; and her five-year-old daughter, Jade, who survived. In addition to the criminal cases, we were also involved in the hearings to sever parental rights of our granddaughter's birth mother and father. Our plan was to adopt Jade so that she would have a family.

Jarred had been the first grandson born into the family. He looked just like his dad. Brian and Melanie were both excited about the birth of their son, while Jade was excited to become a big sister. Unfortunately, it was only about a year after Jarred was born that his parents began to have marital problems. In addition, there were conflicts between Melanie and my husband, who is Brian's father. Melanie didn't want to come to our home or allow the children to come over either. Jarred and Jade became pawns in this situation. At the same time, Jarred and his cousin were very close in age. When the families did come for dinner, Jarred and his cousin would play together. We watched the two of them move through the infant state, to sitting up, to crawling, and to walking. When Jarred was about nineteen months old, I took him and Jade to see Santa Claus. It was the first holiday season that Jarred was aware of Santa Claus and getting gifts. Our precious Jarred was taken from us as a baby, just beginning to understand what the holidays are about.

One day, our main worry was getting our dog's nails cut; the next, our entire lives were changed. A phone call from my husband's ex-wife, telling him that our three-year-old grandson was dying and our five-year-old granddaughter was in the care of Arizona CPS changed our lives. Our daughter-in-law didn't inform any members of the family about the situation. Even when CPS took Jade into custody, Melanie claimed that there wasn't any family in the state who could be contacted.

Again, our law enforcement background was a benefit. My husband contacted the hospital to obtain information regarding Jarred's condition. He also contacted CPS to inquire about the circumstances surrounding Jade's situation and determine what needed to be done to have her taken out of foster care and placed with us. We were able to bring her home within three days. It took a number of years and a toll on the family relationships, but we adopted Jade and have raised her as our own. She is seventeen now and a junior in high school.

Unfortunately, the family scars that this situation left haven't been as successfully healed. After hearing about our situation, someone told me that Jarred was my granddaughter's "Michael," like the angel in the John Travolta movie. She said that she believed Jarred was sent to earth for his three short years so that Jade would have an opportunity to get out of the abusive environment she and Jarred had been subjected to, which took Jarred's life. Jarred was her savior. That analogy was the starting point of the grief process for me, and it has made a difference in being able to work through the grief.

Jade was a ward of the state and then in our custody. During the ensuing years, she received several different types of intensive counseling. When Jade attended her counseling sessions I was often involved and had also read books regarding the grieving and recovery process for these types of situations. I learned that families often bonded together after a crisis, but as time went on that bond often breaks and a wedge will develop—relationships will suffer. There was also information on how differently people handled a crisis years later. Everyone handles grief differently. The time period for grieving varies from person to person. Some people are never able to get past their grief.

Reading about how others handle grief helped me get through the years when our family relationships suffered due to Jarred's brutal murder. In the years following, our family had to deal with his loss; the realization that Jarred and Jade's father was an alcoholic, and that even if no one else understood, our granddaughter's well-being was our number one concern. We could no longer help Jarred, but we could, and would, do everything in our power to insure that Jade had the chance to have a loving, stable life. Unfortunately, the family took sides with the alcoholic father and sympathized with his "victim" attitude. They tried to "help" him through the injustice of losing his daughter and being required to prove himself in order to maintain a relationship with her. They blamed us, and Jade's counselor, for *preventing* Jade from having contact with her father. Everyone seemed to ignore the fact that her father was told he needed to follow certain guidelines in order to build a relationship with his daughter. He was told he needed to visit her on a regular basis and for a specific amount of time, spend time with her doing an activity, and that as his daughter was able to mentally and emotionally deal with the contact, the time and frequency would increase. During his first visit he spent the majority of time talking to his father rather than focusing on his daughter. The next week he was better about spending time with his daughter and talking to her. The third week, he didn't show up. He always had an excuse as to why he couldn't come, why he couldn't follow the counselor's instructions, and why he wouldn't talk to Jade's counselor to determine what was best for his daughter.

Although many years have passed since our angel grandson, Jarred, was murdered, we continue to keep his memory, his life, and his voice in our hearts. We were his voice throughout the court proceedings and sentencing. In the end, both suspects took plea agreements. Jarred's birth mother was sentenced to ten years and was released after having served most of her sentence. She was deported to Germany because she was not a US citizen. Her boyfriend was sentenced to life without parole and remains in prison. Jarred was a wonderful, handsome little guy who was so very loved; the murderer has legal rights, and as the criminal justice process takes place, it sometimes seems those rights take precedence over our loved one, whose rights have been taken away. It is for this reason that we must be Jarred's voice—always.

Nancy Neal

# BRIAN RAY MILLER

## Born: October 1, 1973

### Victim of Homicide: October 19, 1991

Brian was walking his girlfriend home from the bowling alley in our neighborhood of country mailboxes and horse properties in the middle of metropolitan Phoenix. A gunman ran across the street, shooting at their feet as they walked home. Brian walked immediately ahead, leaving his girlfriend, Lisa, behind him, protecting her. The masked gunman demanded his wallet. Brian reached for it, but at the same time asked if he could just keep his driver's license because it had been replaced after being stolen a few weeks before. The gunman, even as Brian was reaching for the wallet, shot him in the shoulder, and as Brian handed him the wallet, shot him in the center of his chest. He never had a chance, falling to the ground immediately. At this time, two other accomplices who were hiding across the street, stood up from behind an electrical box and one of them said, "What'd ya do that for, man?" So we always knew the two who were hiding—though all three were gang members who were bored, broke, and out to rob someone—only expected a robbery, not a murder. When the prosecutor told us he wanted to charge the one they thought was the shooter and have the other two testify to the fact he was the shooter, we were fine with that. The other two plea-bargained to seven years for their testimony. Unfortunately, halfway through the trial, we learned one of the two who was testifying—and had already been sentenced to seven years—was, in fact, the actual shooter. Our prosecutor tried to withdraw from his plea agreement and put him on trial for murder; however, the plea agreement he had accepted was poorly worded and stated that if he testified to who the shooter was, he could not be charged with murder in the case. That meant that even if he had been retried as the shooter, he would have only been given two more years for perjury, in addition to the seven already agreed to. So a cold-blooded killer only served seven years for murdering my son. The killer was eighteen at the time and twenty-five when he got out of prison. Our justice system failed Brian and us.

When Brian's voice was silenced by this brutal murder, I desperately needed to speak for him, about him, and to him. We decided to plant a pine tree in Brian's memory, to care for it and watch it grow, as his life would have grown. Brian's tree became a symbol of his life, growing strong and full, having its own voice in this world. I also began to chronicle my thoughts and feelings as his birthdays passed. I first wrote the following in October of 1995:

## Brian's Tree

Today should have been my son's twenty-second birthday. Instead, I stand barefoot among the grasses, tenderly caressing the silken needles of the pine tree planted in his memory several years ago. The tiny, brown pinecones scattered sparingly on the tips of its branches remind me of long ago, and the infant child then growing in my womb. Salty tears mingle with a tender smile—oh, so bittersweet.

Painful memories entwine with sweet ones as I admire this tree. Its growth represents a circle of life. Brian's tree is taller than my husband, who is six inches over six feet. It is growing sturdy, straight, and beautiful, as our son once grew. The irony of my thoughts does not escape me as I lightly caress, desperately searching for the beauty—silent, invisible hope—among the branches. I search for it daily in my struggle to survive the endless sorrow of my aching heart. Sunlight streams through the spaces between each branch, creating a special glow that matches my mood, and yet, mocks it—oh, so bittersweet.

Christmas 1991—six weeks after Brian was killed—already it seems a lifetime of tears, shattered dreams, and horror. I always refer to my son as killed. You die of accident, illness, or normal aging. Brian did not simply die. My son was murdered. Such a horrible word, and yet no aesthetic sugarcoating can gentle it. No other word can do justice to the reality of it. It was horrible what happened to our son—to us. We planted a tree that first Christmas without him. We knew nothing else to do to ease the pain.

Still in shock, we did not yet realize the full implications of living without him.

Yet we have carried on. All the repercussions of his death have not left us totally filled with hate, despair, and bitterness, or devoid of joy. I still believe in the overall good and beauty in life perfectly demonstrated in this tree. We were lucky, my family and I, to see much compassion from caring people in our lives and our neighborhood. *Lucky* seems an odd word to use when you have suffered the worst that life can offer. Compassionate people, a side of tragic events that gives us hope despite the darkness—the good that comes even out of darkest evil. However, we hurt. We are angry at times. We anguish and suffer—like today. We always will.

As I bask in the warmth of the sun streaming through the branches, reaching toward the heavens, I think of this tree. Strong roots give it life. The same as the cord attached to my infant son, giving him life before his birth. A cord severed by birth—physically— but never emotionally. A mother's bond transplanted now in nurturing this representation of what once was in my life, now only in my heart. It feels good to grow and nurture. After all, that is what motherhood is about. This tree does not take his place, and yet I water, feed, and relish the fact that it is flourishing with my attentions, despite the wrath of desert summers in Phoenix.

As Brian's tree flourishes, it reminds me that I can too, in spite of a broken heart that will never totally heal; in spite of a family left behind like a jigsaw puzzle in jagged pieces. We have put the puzzle together again with much diligence and hard work because of our love and commitment to each other. And yet a part of the whole picture is missing. We can never piece it together completely, and the road of grief we travel sometimes causes the pieces to become displaced again and again. I am confident we can put them together as many times as it takes. What is left of the puzzle with the missing piece is still a family. Recent family pictures are bittersweet reminders of this fact. We smile. We are three—Don, Christie, and me. In our hearts and memories though, we will always be four.

"Hello, Brian's tree. You look beautiful today." Briefly during this conversation, I worry what someone passing might think—then realize—I do not care. I have earned my right through enduring incredible pain; and grief allows me the freedom to talk to myself and to this tree. "Happy Birthday, dearest son." Oh God, please let the magic of sweet memories of our life together and the beauty in this tree always console us. Please allow another anniversary to pass, not without pain—it never will—but simply without further trauma to my family and myself.

October 2000: Today should have been my son's twenty-seventh birthday. I once again spend it admiring his tree, but oh, how it has grown, towering toward the sky above, three times as tall as my husband now. Salty tears mingle with smiles as I recall the precious times we once shared together, and the times we will not share again. Four years ago we adopted a baby girl. She will never know her brother. Our two grandsons born since, Brandon and Dillon, will never know their uncle. Oh, so bittersweet!

Life goes on. We went from being simply survivors, as we survived just by breathing and getting out of bed each morning. I wanted to not only survive my son's murder, but live life fully in spite of it. It was not an easy journey, but we have traveled it. My family, in our hearts and memories, are now always five. One always missing from current family pictures—Don, Christie, Kimberlie, and me—Brian always in our hearts.

October 2001: Another today, another milestone marked with what should have been Brian's twenty-eighth birthday. I cannot help, in tender melancholy, but reflect on what would…should, have been. How many children would he have now? Would he be dreading his birthday, the next to the last of his twenties before the decade of his thirties began?

I have seen most of his friends get married; many have at least two children now. As much as Brian loved kids, I would like to think, had he lived, he would have more. The grandchildren of my dreams. The other grandchildren I was cheated out of, though I thank God for the two I do have from my daughter. Bittersweet memories of what I have and what I don't. I would love for one sweet and precious thing in my life, since his death, which is to not have to be entwined, like the branches on his tree, with the bitterness. Alas, it cannot be. I pray for the strength to continue the constant battle to not let the bitterness overcome the sweet. It is a choice and I have to recommit to it often, especially on birthdays and anniversaries—stark reminders of what was taken from us.

In the beginning I thought the pain would kill me. I also thought someday the pain would end because I was in shock and I hurt so badly that I could not envision that pain for a lifetime. Foolish me. One day I finally realized I was never getting over the murder of my son. In that realization, though, came my stark determination to live with it by giving meaning to living with it. I have succeeded. I have failed. Oh, so bittersweet.

"Hello, Brian's tree. You look beautiful today, though not as straight as you once grew. From one angle you are gently swayed as if you had weathered a storm. If I could not bend with the storms of my continuing battle of living with your murder, I would not be here now."

October 2003: Dearest son, you would be thirty this year. How can I have a child of thirty? How can you be making me older when you are no longer in my life? How did twelve years dare to pass without you sharing our family milestones? I miss you as much today as yesterday, as much twelve years later as one minute after we left the hospital where I held your cold, lifeless body and begged you to open your eyes; where I begged God to give you back to me—to us. I want you other than in spirit, other than tucked safely in loving memories, and other than in dreams.

I am proud of how your dad and I are still helping others who travel this same journey of indescribable pain and loss. Your sister, Christie, now co-facilitates our Teen Group with our counselor. Kimberlie, now seven, the sister who never knew you other than through us, now grieves for you, too. Her emotional investment in the brother she has never known personally makes her feel cheated. She is angry you cannot come back from heaven. We are a family, though, changed for the better and sometimes the worse, but a family nonetheless.

Thank you to all who helped me survive. As I will inevitably stand on these grasses many more times on other birthdays and anniversaries without him, and as love never ends, let this tree never die…

"I love you, Brian."

May the same strong roots giving life to this tree continue to give life to us.

October 1, 2006, would have been your thirty-third birthday. Time marches on and yet you remain forever eighteen in our minds and hearts. You are young forever, my dearest son. I wish I could see a picture of you, who you'd be today. Would it hurt more to see what we have missed?

I have begun a new tradition with the tree planted in your memory that towers high, reaching for the clouds. Each October I find a tiny pinecone and place it in a basket of other pinecones collected through the years. Collecting memories and mementos, reaching out to touch you in some way—reminders of you. Not enough and yet so much. It is all I have. I miss you more with each passing year. I always will.

October 1, 2010, and what would be your thirty-eighth birthday had you lived; instead, it's your nineteenth birthday in heaven.

We moved and had to leave Brian's tree behind, though I can still see it from where we are living now…bittersweet. I wonder whether the people who move there will take care of the tree as I did, and yet I know they will have no emotional investment in it. People ask how I can leave it. I must, as it is too tall for transplanting.

It was planted for a reason all those years ago, when we knew not what to do. Our grief and pain was so overwhelming, our life in such upheaval. It is okay now to leave the tree as it served its purpose and more for many years. It will live forever in my memories, as does my son. No one can take those away. It is a reminder of the strength of our family in surviving the nightmare of his death. We have fallen again and again, faced the battering of storms, taken just as many, if not more, steps backward as forward, and yet we remain a strong family. Brian is always in our hearts and his tree will always live there, too.

Beckie A. Miller

# Ronald Allen Fraga

## Born: July 7, 1990

### Victim of Homicide: January 12, 2008

Ronnie was my first grandchild. There were two people with him when he came into this world, and two when he went out: his mother, Amy, and myself—Gloria. We had gone out to dinner to celebrate January birthdays at Texas Roadhouse. We only had one car to transport thirteen people. Ronnie and his brother Mitchell, Aunt Amber, friends Joshua and Nageb, went home on the first trip. While I went back to the restaurant to pick up the others, there were some boys walking down the street, throwing beer bottles at the house. Mitchell went out to confront them and was arguing with them. They were across the street, which is a four-lane road.

Ronnie poked his head out the bedroom window to see what was going on and saw his brother arguing with the boys. He jumped out of the window to defend his brother. When he went outside, the confrontation escalated. Ronnie sent his brother to "get the heat." We assume he meant a gun, but none was ever found. We think he did this to get his brother out of harm's way.

Three of the four or five in the group came across the street brandishing a knife, while Ronnie picked up a skateboard to defend himself.

Amber called to tell us there was a fight and to get home fast. We told her to tell them to stop and we would handle it when we got home. When she said, "It is not our boys," we told her to call 911. Ronnie shouted to Amber to get into the house because she was pregnant. At the same time, she was trying to get him in the house away from danger. He then stumbled in and said, "Those fools stabbed me," and went to get towels from the bathroom. Ronnie collapsed on the couch, where we found him. His mother went to his left side, I to his right side. Amy held his hand and told him to hang on, to think about Jessica and Joey, and that he was loved and needed. Then my daughter took a deep breath and said, "Ronnie, you do what you need to do. Jessica and Joey will be fine." He then squeezed her hand and let go. All I could do was put my hand on him and say one word: "Jesus." I could not find the words to pray, but I know that Jesus was with me and was holding my family at that point. I was numb because I had just watched my baby grandson leave this life. No, it was not official, and I did not want to believe it, but as a nurse, I knew what had just happened. And the nightmare began.

Ronnie left behind a seven-month-old son, Joey; his girlfriend, Jessica; mother, Amy; sister, Azura; brother, Mitchell; Aunt Amber; Aunt Daneer; Uncle Ian; father, Ron; grandmother, Wanda; Aunt Vinnie;

Aunt Ronda; and myself, grandmother, Gloria. The next few days were a nightmarish blur with the funeral and all the calls, people coming over, all the food…it was so overwhelming at times that I just wanted to be alone to get my mind straight to grieve for Ronnie. It was not to be because so much needed to be done and I did not know where to start. Amy was so deep in her grief that she could not function. What a lot of people do not know is that I lost two people that night, because the person Amy was no longer existed. She could not, and still can't, be alone. She was lost for a very long time, often forgetting everything else and everyone around her because if she was awake she had to deal with Ronnie never coming home, never telling her he loved her, never waking her up to take him to work for 7:00 a.m., even though it was only 5:00 a.m. He did not like to be late for anything. Never again would I hear him ask for money for Taco Bell, never again to take off in my car in the middle of the night.

It took fifteen months to make an arrest. DNA was sent back five times before they identified it. On May 6, 2009, Manuel Morado was arrested. I had called to talk to the detective and was told he could not talk to me because I was not a victim, and he was unable to tell me anything. I loved Ronnie. He was my first grandchild—I saw him come into this world, and I was with him when he left. How could the detective say I was not a victim? I was hurting badly and there was nobody to talk to. I was a victim twice: I lost my daughter and Ronnie. I lost Amy to a deep depression that she still has not come back from, and I lost Ronnie to death. How could he say I was not a victim?

The first trial date was so hard. I saw the person responsible for taking Ronnie from us. I wanted to jump over the spectator's bench and beat him, make him hurt like he did Ronnie, but that would not have solved anything. I was at every court date I could possibly attend. I could not say to the murderer what I wanted to say. I wanted to be Ronnie's voice. I felt robbed of a normal life since life cannot be normal without Ronnie. I miss him more than anyone can say or truly understand. I was not his mother; I was his grandmother who loved him more than life itself. His right to live and be a father to his baby son was taken away by Manuel Morado, who was sentenced to thirteen years, with credit for 429 days time served.

I was asked where my God was now. Why did He not prevent this, and the answer came to me. "He is right here next to me. He is holding me up; He is giving me the strength to get through this." I know Ronnie is in a better place. He is sitting at the right hand of God. He is not hurting anymore and has gone home to heaven. Without God and Jesus I would not get through this each day. When I need strength I just pray, and somehow I am able to make it through the day. I am asking to grant forgiveness, but I'm not sure I can. All I can do is continue to ask God, "Help me forgive this person." Sometimes I hope I will be able to.

Gloria Brown

# Kristin Laurite

## Born: January 28, 1975

### Victim of Homicide: August 25, 2000

On August 25, 2000, my life changed forever. My beautiful twenty-five-year-old daughter, Kristin, was brutally raped and murdered at a rest stop in Morrillton, Arkansas. Kristin was stabbed eleven times in the neck in the light of day by a serial killer, Ronald Ward. She was the first of four known victims murdered by Ward. Kristin had parked at the rest stop that afternoon to take a break from driving, cool down her van, and give her beloved dogs, Sativa and Winter, a chance to exercise. Evidently, Ronald Ward happened upon my daughter, and she became his first victim in a string of murders. Five horrendous years passed before her killer was identified. Finally, in 2005, DNA evidence was traced to Ronald Ward.

We discovered that Ronald Ward had been incarcerated since January of 2001 for the murder of a homeless man in Montana in October 2000. Due to the backlog of DNA testing and human error, it took five years to identify Kristin's killer. Unfortunately, Ronald

Ward's DNA was never entered into the CODIS system when he was arrested, which greatly delayed solving Kristin's murder. Legislation needs to be passed in every state, mandating that DNA be processed for all felons and put into the database.

Kristin was traveling to Eureka, California, with her two companions, Sativa and Winter, to settle down. She had put a deposit on a rental house there and was very anxious to start a new chapter in life on the west coast. She adored children and was planning to work as a teacher. But that dream would never be realized.

Vibrant and high spirited, Kristin lived and enjoyed life to its fullest. She was not your average person because she did not conform to the norm in her dress, ambition, and philosophies. As a young child, she was extremely independent, and she died the same way. Her work ethic was strong, as well as her convictions. She was extremely passionate about protecting the environment and had an enormous love for animals. Kristin's determination was fierce to achieve her goals, and she let nothing stand in her way. It was ironic that, on the day that Kristin was leaving home for her journey to California, she confided that she had an ominous feeling about the trip. In fact, she left and returned home before leaving for good.

Years ago, Kristin had babysat for the daughter of a family friend, Leslie Gleason. After Kristin's death, Leslie reflected on my daughter, describing her perfectly:

"Kristin seemed to be composed entirely of bones and joints, sparkling eyes, immense smiles, exuberant hair, and pure, raw energy. She almost seemed to emit energy like an electrical current. She vibrated with life. There was nothing ordinary about Kristin. She didn't have average views and opinions, or average tastes, or an average philosophy, or average jobs, or average friendships. She was true and completely extraordinary. Even if you didn't share her level of passionate commitment to her views and beliefs, you had to admire the passion of her own dedication. She was an influence that I always felt lucky to have in my daughter Shayna's life."

No words can sufficiently describe the anguish and pain a parent feels after losing a child; and to have your child taken away by such a brutal and senseless act only adds to your agonizing grief. The fact that you have lost your child at the hands of someone who purposefully harmed her intensifies the pain you are going through to the point where it becomes paralyzing. It is not the natural order of life to outlive your child. The love a mother has for her child is overpowering and unique… if only I could have traded places with my daughter.

My life has forever been changed due to this violent and brutal act. Kristin was my only child, and I miss her every minute of every day. There is a tremendous void in my life that can never be filled. The sadness I feel is so overwhelming at times that I do not want to go on. The support of my family and friends has allowed me to survive. During the long five years between the time

Kristin was murdered and the killer was found, we were in frequent contact with the authorities in Arkansas. My sister, especially, was unrelenting in finding this serial killer.

All who loved Kristin have been greatly affected by her death. Her young friends were traumatized by her murder and will never be quite the same. My family members now fear for the safety of their own children as a result of Kristin's brutal death.

My faith has also allowed me to survive my horrific loss. Although I am not a churchgoer, I do believe that God will correct the evils that exist, and that we will someday be reunited with our loved ones.

The ache in my heart is constant since the loss of my Kristin. However, I know she would want me to enjoy what life still has to offer. Her two dogs, Sativa and Winter, have lived with me since her death. They were instrumental in discovering she had been murdered and in finding her body. A truck driver who had also stopped at the rest area was constantly followed by Winter until he took notice. He called me using the phone number on Winter's collar, explaining the situation. With this information, I called the authorities in Morrillton, asking them to search for Kristin. When they found her, Sativa was lying next to her body. Even though the truck driver and his wife were heading to the west coast, they took the dogs with them and then brought them to their home in Tennessee. I flew to Tennessee to pick up Kristin's dogs and drove them back to my home in New Jersey. I so appreciate the couple's kindness, and the fact that they questioned why the dog was milling around Kristin's van that day. If not for their awareness, crucial DNA evidence would have been lost due to the extreme heat on the day Kristin was killed. So the actions of various people and two devoted animal friends ultimately led to the discovery of my daughter's body and to the killer responsible for her death. Sativa and Winter gave me a purpose to go on and have comforted me throughout the grieving process, as they were such a part of my daughter. In January of 2010 Sativa died, which proved to be devastating. Winter passed away in 2011. It was as if I still had a piece of Kristin while they lived, and now I have lost that part of her all over again.

I am one of the lucky ones who saw justice for my daughter's murder. Not everyone is that fortunate. Although it brought me peace of mind that this monster had been caught, it can never take away the devastation that he inflicted upon my family and me. He will spend the rest of his life in prison, but he still has a life. When he took my daughter's life, he sentenced me to life without my beautiful Kristin. I will always be Kristin's voice; she will always be remembered and loved.

My heart goes out to all those who have lost a loved one through violence. I know the feeling every day of my life.

Lynn McMahon

# Ruth Angel Hayes

## Born: February 6, 1979

### Victim of Homicide: January 27, 2007

My daughter, Ruth Angel Hayes, was murdered on January 27, 2007. On that day I learned what true, heart-wrenching grief is about. Angel was a wonderful, much loved young woman with everything to live for. She had a son who she was raising to be a responsible young man, and she was in preparation to welcome her second child. At the time of her murder, Angel was happily three months pregnant. My daughter was an excellent mother—always interested in her son's progress at school, always working hard to make their lives even better. Now, I raise my grandson and do my best to carry on the way I know my Angel would have for her son.

I said Angel always worked hard to make life better for her son and her unborn baby. When she had decided that it would be best for her family to end her relationship with her children's father, she had obtained a restraining order. He was very jealous and controlling. She did not feel safe around him. In fact, the day before

Angel was killed by multiple shotgun blasts, she gave me important papers to keep, and though she did not say so, it was as if she felt something would happen.

The day Angel was murdered I had called her when I got home from work. She told me that she was tired. I had made plans to go to the casino with my sister. While there, I had a bad feeling. Then I got a call on my cell phone telling me that my daughter had been shot. I was frantic at this point, not knowing whether Angel was still alive or how seriously she was hurt. I asked my sister to take me to the hospital, but by the time we arrived, Angel had died of her injuries. My grandson was at the scene when his mother was killed. He had run to my house, but, of course, I wasn't home.

Angel and the killer had been in a relationship for seven years. He didn't want her to speak to anyone and suspected that everyone was trying to break them up. After he shot my daughter, he disappeared. Due to the publicity of Angel's murder being shown on America's Most Wanted, the efforts of the FBI, the Philadelphia Police Crime Stoppers program and the reward that they offered, along with the help of so many wonderful people, this fugitive killer was caught right before Father's Day in 2007. He had been on the run about six months.

He was convicted of murder after many court appearances, which I attended. I had to be there for my daughter; she could no longer speak for herself or her child. When he was sentenced to two life sentences, his mother spoke up, saying that she "wouldn't be able to see my son...he's going to prison." I gave my impact statement. I said that I would never see my Angel and my grandchild. I asked him why he had to kill her. As I was saying this, the murderer sat there smiling in the courtroom.

My daughter's murder has left me angry, sad, and grief-stricken, but counseling is helping me. I can never forget what has happened to my Angel, even though people think I should be *over it*. They tell me to *move on*. What they don't realize is that God does move me on...in His time. He has given me a counselor to help me through this, but *get over it* and *move on* are not in my vocabulary right now. People mean well, but they can't possibly understand what I go through every day of my life now that my daughter's violent death has shattered my life and the life of my grandson. He suffers in school with bullying and teasing. I am his champion now that his mom is gone, and I ask for support from the school administration.

We were a loving, close family. Angel has an older brother and a younger sister; they share my grief. If not for my faith in God I don't know what would have happened to my grandson and myself since my daughter was killed. My sister, who I was with the day Angel was shot, has not called me or seen me since that time. I don't understand this, although I do know that many people feel uncomfortable around me in my grief.

Angel was always looking up; she was a graduate of Overbrook High School and attended Community College of Philadelphia before starting the Professional

Nursing School of Philadelphia. She was a model student in school. Angel would do anything for anyone. She so looked forward to her new baby and was hoping for a girl—a sister for her beloved son. My daughter worked hard to give her son a good life. She worked in the Philadelphia Airport, at JC Penney, and at the Philadelphia Housing Authority. Angel was well loved and respected by her co-workers and friends. The staff of the Philadelphia Museum of Art had a portrait made of her. When they presented the portrait to me, it felt like proof of how much Angel meant to so many in her life.

There were so many wonderful people who helped us during the time that the murderer was a fugitive. The friends at my job and my Angel's job who sent cards and prayers were so thoughtful. The witness who helped to get the murderer caught will forever be in my prayers. People who I didn't even know, but who knew Angel, were so helpful. I want all of these people, and my family and friends to know how thankful I am for them, that they were here for me during the hardest time in my life.

It has been on my mind for a long time to give the public some information that I feel is so important. We need to continue working on getting guns off the street. Go to war if you must kill; if you can't handle things, talk about it. If a person wants to be away from you, let them go. When a child is born to us, we must understand that this is a gift. No one has the right to take a life; show love to family readily…give hugs, send cards, show and tell love to family. Each child is special—you must love your children and show it, not give *things* in place of love. Maybe if the parents of the one who murdered my Angel had raised their son with love and faith, he wouldn't have grown up to be a needy person who felt he had to control those in his life. Maybe he wouldn't have taken a gun and killed my daughter.

Really think about the words of this book and listen to the words so your heart can be filled. Know that if our children were here they would tell you the same. Hear our children's voices.

Ruth E. Hayes

# EPILOGUE

It is impossible to know what it is like to lose a loved one to murder unless you have lived through the anguish of this experience. Many of the stories included in this book have been written by parents who have lost their child to murder; however, grandparents, siblings, and spouses have all been affected by the murder of their loved ones. No one who has any connection to the victim escapes the tragic effects of murder. Suffering the loss of loved ones through illness, accident, or other tragedies are certainly experiences filled with sorrow. Add to that the dimension of dealing with the reality that someone intended to kill your loved one. Someone not only did not care about his or her right to live, but forcibly took that right away. It is critically important for the criminal justice system to understand victim's rights and to work toward insuring that the rights of the victim are, at the very least, equal to the rights of the accused. Instead, the rights of victims and co-victims become lost in a system geared to guaranteeing the rights of the accused. The laws that govern our criminal justice system become a farce when murderers are granted repeated appeals. The cost, financially and emotionally, to society in general and to co-victims in particular, is staggering.

Victims of homicide must have a representative to be their voice. Victims have no appeals, no pleas, and no choices. Please hear their voices. Though they have been silenced, they cry out to be heard. Victim's rights have fallen on hard times in many states as pressing economic issues have consumed the time and energy of our legislators. We can all help ensure that victim's rights remain in the forefront of our national awareness by keeping our eyes and ears open. When we hear or read of legislation regarding the rights of victims being stalled, we must contact our senators, assembly people, and representatives. We must tell them how important it is to place victims' rights first.

Legislation introduced by a co-victim or an interested government entity, designed to address injustices, goes a long way toward giving silenced victims a voice, while saving uncounted potential victims. Maggie's Law, introduced by Carole McDonnell, whose daughter was a victim of vehicular homicide, seeks to prevent driving while drowsy. The law carries a fine and jail time. Gregory's Law, introduced by Cathy Katsnelson, whose son was a victim of a diagnosed schizophrenic, makes court ordered outpatient treatment mandatory for those with diagnosed mental illness. Megan's Law, introduced by Maureen Kanka, whose daughter was the victim of a sex offender, identifies and makes the public aware of the location of convicted sex offenders who live in the area. Caylee's

Law is a bill which has recently been introduced in many states. It would require that children who go missing must be reported to the authorities in a timely manner. The impetus of this bill is the Caylee Marie Anthony case. Caylee, three years old, was missing for a month before police were notified. Her remains were not found until six months later. At that point, authorities were unable to determine a cause of death. Over time, our laws have evolved in response to the needs of our society. Let's be our loved ones' voices, loud and clear. Let's honor our silenced ones through continuing the fight for victims' rights.

# Resources

The following are organizations to contact for help and support:

Angelmoms.com
   An Internet community of bereaved mothers
   of children of all ages and causes of death.
   www.angelmoms.com

Anti-Violence Partnership of Philadelphia, PA.
   For Families of Murder Victims (FMV)
   Committed to helping co-victims of homicide by
   providing criminal justice information,
   emotional support and trial accompaniment.
   215-686-8033 www.avpphila.org/fmv.html

Bereaved Parents of the USA (BP/USA)
   Offers support, understanding, compassion and
   hope especially to the newly bereaved.
   www.bereavedparentsusa.org

The Center for Victims of Violence and Crime (CVVC)
24-Hour Helpline: 412-392-8582
Located in Pittsburgh, PA. Community-based,
its mission is to heal trauma, resolve conflict, and
end violence.
www.cvvc.org

The Compassionate Friends (TCF)
Supports and assists bereaved parents, siblings, and
other family members in the positive resolution
of their grief, and to foster their physical and
emotional health.
www.thecompassionatefriendsfw.com

Family and Friends of Violent Crime Victims
A crime victims' service center in Washington.
Provides Victim Advocates to those whose lives
have been devastated by violent crime.
www.fnfvcv.org

GriefNet
An Internet community of persons dealing with
grief, death, and major loss.
www.GriefNet.org

Memorial Wall for Murder Victims
Created in remembrance of our loved ones who
were murdered, as well as to show visitors the
reality that survivors must live with.
www.murdervictimsmemorialwall.com

MurderVictims.com
> A memorial to the innocent victims of violent crime and a source of help for murder victim survivors. The focus is on the victims of the most violent of crimes: murder. Co-victims can come here for help, to ask questions, give and get advice.
> www.murdervictims.com

National Center for Victims of Crime (NCVC)
> Encourages public awareness of crime victim issues in local communities throughout the country.
> www.ncvc.org

National Organization for Victim Assistance (NOVA)
> Promotes rights and services for victims of crime and crisis everywhere.
> www.trynova.org

POMC (Parents of Murdered Children)
> For the families of those who have died by violence. Offers various types of assistance and support.
> 100 East Eighth Street, Suite 202
> Cincinnati, Ohio 45202
> www.pomc.com

This brief list is given to assist co-victims in finding support. Many of these sites will offer links to other resources.

Justice will only be achieved when those who are not injured by crime feel as indignant as those who are.

King Solomon

# THE UNDEFENDED VICTIM

For me, no gavel hammers,

The scales were never weighed,

My crime was that of victim,

My life was the price I paid.

And when my life was taken,

Why weren't my rights read?

And the statement "overruled,"

When they pronounced me dead?

I'll never hear my rights,

Nor take the witness stand,

No attorney to defend me,

My fate was in a killer's hands.

Now the courtroom's crowded,

As the defendant pleads the case,

With just a glimmer of a tear,

Cold eyes on a straight face.

But oh, that I could take the stand,

If they could witness my last breath,

Could they live with the terror,

That I went through in death.

If they could hear my pleading cries,

And see the hatred in that face,

At last, we'd know, the scales had

"Been balanced" in this case.

If I could, I'd tell the jury

Exactly how it was,

The fear and pain I went through,

Struck down without a cause.

Did they carefully weigh it all

As they listened to the plea?

There were no emotions showing now,

Just the hope of going free.

The final verdict now is in,

As the defendant stands in tears,

If only I had done as well…

Given ten to twenty years.

Author Unknown

# e|LIVE

## listen|imagine|view|experience

### AUDIO BOOK DOWNLOAD INCLUDED WITH THIS BOOK!

In your hands you hold a complete digital entertainment package. In addition to the paper version, you receive a free download of the audio version of this book. Simply use the code listed below when visiting our website. Once downloaded to your computer, you can listen to the book through your computer's speakers, burn it to an audio CD or save the file to your portable music device (such as Apple's popular iPod) and listen on the go!

How to get your free audio book digital download:

1. Visit www.tatepublishing.com and click on the e|LIVE logo on the home page.
2. Enter the following coupon code:
   63c6-a0cd-65e4-3f0e-e3e5-d81b-9f4d-4211
3. Download the audio book from your e|LIVE digital locker and begin enjoying your new digital entertainment package today!